WISDOM FROM
THE DEEP LIVING BLOG

ALSO BY SUSANNE MEYER-FITZSIMMONS

Deep Living: Healing Yourself To Heal The Planet

PRAISE FOR DEEP LIVING

"My 21st century lifestyle is a fast-paced and frenetic one. I've looked forward to Susanne's blog for years to get me 'back on track.' She has the keen ability to express in words my thoughts and feelings about living more deeply. Each blog is a meditation about living well, eating well, and feeling well—'short and sweet,' yet substantive in so many ways."

—*Annette Sanchez, educator*

"I've always felt that a collective of individuals contributing in small ways to improving the human condition is the construct of a movement. . . . Susanne's work reminds us what each of us can do, how each one of us can make a difference."

—*Steve Rubin, Director of The Hudson Valley Jazz Festival*

"Susanne's concise Deep Living blog posts encourage us to re-discover and celebrate the magic in simple, everyday observations. An unexpected sign on a road trip invites reflection, 'This building is not empty. It is full of opportunity!' Her sources of inspiration are varied. Sometimes, the animals who we share the Earth with, are featured. Did you know octopi can distinguish between people the like or dislike? Have you ever wondered about communicating telepathically with your pets?"

—*Alice Longworth, marketing executive*

WISDOM FROM
THE DEEP LIVING BLOG

A Deep Living Companion Book

SUSANNE MEYER-FITZSIMMONS

FCP

Full Court Press
Englewood Cliffs, New Jersey

First Edition

Published in the United States of America
by Full Court Press, 601 Palisade Avenue,
Englewood Cliffs, NJ 07632
fullcourtpressnj.com

ISBN 978-1-946989-05-5
Library of Congress Catalog No. 2017958511

Editing and book design by Barry Sheinkopf for Bookshapers
(bookshapers.com)

Illustrations by Catherine Pierson DeCesare
(31high.com)

Covert Art by Caroline Siecke-Pape

To Gaia, our dear planet Earth

*May she forgive us for all our experimenting
and show us the way back.
Without her we do not exist.*

DISCLAIMER

Because of the dynamic nature of the internet, any web addresses or links contained in this book may have changed since publication and may no longer be valid.

The views expressed in this book are solely those of the author and do not necessarily reflect the views of the publisher, and the publisher hereby disclaims any responsibility for them.

The author of this book does not dispense medical advice or prescribe the use of any technique as a form of treatment for physical, emotional, or medical problems without the advice of a physician, either directly or indirectly. The intent of the author is only to offer information of a general nature to help you in your quest for emotional and spiritual wellbeing. In the event you use any of the information in this book for yourself, which is your constitutional right, the author and the publisher assume no responsibility for your actions.

FOREWORD

In March of 2012, a month before I was awarded my master's degree, I started the Holistic Living Blog as a way of building an online voice and presence. The degree had become a research platform and basis for *Deep Living: Healing Yourself To Heal The Planet*, my first book, which was published at the beginning of this year and can be viewed as the long form of the blog. Now, almost six years later, I have attracted a steady following of faithful blog readers and created a library of many hundreds of blog posts that have become a thought provoking body of writing in its own right. This summer Feedspot nominated the blog one of the top one hundred holistic blogs on the web.

May this compilation of short reflections provide you with bursts of inspiration and show you how magical everyday life can be, how good-for-all and not just good-for-some, if you live more deeply.

—*S.M-F.,*
Warwick, August 2017

ACKNOWLEDGMENTS

I am grateful—for my husband Brian's unwavering support of my writing endeavors and his push to get this book, which has hung in limbo in cyberspace, out the door; for all the kind and encouraging thoughts about this blog from readers Annette Sanchez, Steve Rubin, Gary Bilezikian, Beverly Braxton, and Alice Longworth; for my yoga teacher Aura Lehrer's many oh-so-spiritual remarks during her yoga sessions that have inspired many a blog post; for my children Nicholas and Zoë, who inspired quite a few posts as well; for Catherine Pierson DeCesare's beautiful jewel-like divider page icons (I finally got the opportunity to work with her); for Caroline Siecke-Pape's original *Deep Living* cover illustration that made it, in a new color scheme, onto this second book; for my beautiful life and the terrific community I have the privilege to live in, and that brings me inspiration for blogging all day long; for Barry Sheinkopf, who did it again— counseling, editing, designing, producing, eBooking, and getting this book to the table; and lastly, for all my readers, present and future— thank you for following me, an author is nothing without an audience.

.

TABLE OF CONTENTS

*Thoughts on
communicating compassionately*

Anti-war or pro-peace?   April 30, 2013

Perhaps surprisingly it's not the same! It is not the same to be anti big-ag or anti-pesticides or pro-organic. It's not the same to be anti-abortion or pro-life. Energetically being anti anything perpetuates that which we protest, since that is what we keep thinking about (the energy doesn't get the "not" part). If you keep protesting against war, war is the energy that gets perpetuated, whereas if you lobby for peace, peace is the energy that is being strengthened. Being pro something turns our mind to that which we favor, that which we wish to manifest. That's why it is so important to formulate what you *do* want in life, not what you *don't* want, although defining first what you *don't* want helps you to define better what it is you actually *do* want.

So next time you are angry with something out there—perhaps the politicians, the terrible meat industry, your co-worker, your child for something s/he did—turn your thinking around and emphasize what you'd like to see instead: Vote *for* something, buy meat that has been raised the way you prefer, talk to your co-worker about the feelings her behavior elicits in you and what can be done about it, encourage and reward your child for the behavior you'd like to reinforce.

Life is here to make you better   October 1, 2013

"Life is here to make you better, not bitter," said my yoga teacher the other day. It's important to realize that people don't do or say things to annoy you. People do whatever they do, and say whatever they say, from the perspective of their own emotional needs.

We all have common universal emotional needs, such as the needs for love, shelter, safety, nourishment, sleep; and we have more individualistic emotional needs for say beauty, peace, creativity, order, quiet, connection, community, and so on.

We usually operate in an egocentric world and thus live from the perspective of our individual needs. When those needs are not recognized or met we tend to get irritated, annoyed, impatient, angry, or even furious. These emotions signal our own, not the other person's, unmet needs.

When my daughter does her math homework slowly, methodically, not too neatly, I tend to become impatient and raise the tone of my voice. That signals my unmet need for neatness and organization, and my self-imposed desire to get on with it, and on to other activities. I need to remind myself that I irritate myself, my daughter doesn't irritate me.

So, instead of becoming bitter at others for supposedly annoying me all day long, hassling me, wanting to irritate and frustrate me, bitter at what life throws in my way, let me dig a bit deeper into those emotions. Let them make me better, more compassionate and understanding.

Right or wrong   April 24, 2014

We easily tend to judge something as right or wrong—after all we live in a dualistic world and can't avoid seeing our existence through juxtapositions. Good and bad, black and white, cold and warm. It seems only natural to take sides, argue, condemn, judge, and feel bad when someone doesn't share my opinion. But it helps to see the other person's perspective to understand how silly some arguments are, and how what we thought was "wrong" ends up being "right" from a different viewpoint. Let me put that into perspective.

A few years ago my sister and I had a discussion over towel drying logistics—this was before I stopped using my clothes dryer. I argued that dryer-dried towels felt so good because they were soft, which conveyed to me the feeling of "freshly washed." "On the contrary," my sister, who doesn't have a dryer, said (most Europeans actually don't). Her scratchy and stiff line-dried towels give her that feeling of "freshly laundered," she explained, because soft towels leave the impression that they have been used and need to be washed. Okay, point well taken.

A few years later, when energy costs went through the roof, I woke up and stopped using my drier in favor of drying racks (air and sunshine are for free, electricity is not)— —and lo and behold, my attitude changed 180° and I found myself adopting her position.

Wars are fought over such "rights" and "wrongs." We know the familiar arguments over toothpaste tube rolling up, or not, and how to insert the toilet paper roll into the holder, with the paper down the front or the back. Try putting yourself in the other shoes next time you are ready to judge a person for their nose ring, their opinion, their hair color (blue anyone?), or their religion.

My favorite word is "sure"   May 16, 2014

That's what my friend said a few days ago. And she is right. Can you imagine how easy your life became if everyone of your requests was answered with "sure?"

Imagine you asked your son to clean up his room and put away his clothes, and he replied, "Sure."

Imagine you asked your co-worker to help you figure out some computer problem that has been bugging you for days, and she answered, "Sure."

Imagine you called the plumber to fix your leaky faucet and asked him whether he could come tonight after five, and he said, "Sure."

Imagine you asked your boss for a reasonable and well-earned raise, and she simply said, "Sure."

Imagine you asked a friend to help you move a heavy item over the weekend, and he said, "Sure."

Yesterday afternoon I was relaxing with the newspaper. I had about fifteen minutes before I needed to get dinner going, in time to leave for an evening meeting. Just then my daughter asked for help pulling her spring clothes down, and putting her winter clothes up and away, something we had been wanting to do for a few days. I grumbled something, I didn't want to be bothered, I stuck my head back into the paper, and then I remembered that little magical word "sure"...and got up to help her. She was so happy and surprised and said, "I thought you weren't gonna help me."

By saying "sure," you say "yes" to life.

The war against evil?   July 8, 2014

Have you ever wondered why there is so much warfare, strife, and conflict out there? Mother Teresa supposedly replied to an invitation to participate in an anti-war demonstration with, "You can invite me when you are planning a pro-peace event." The perspective is fundamentally different.

Ask yourself how you think. We tend to be *against* certain politics, *hate* so-and-so, *dislike* fish, *mind* the rain, *despise* the humidity, or have a dust allergy. In summary, we very much know everything we *don't* like. The problem with that perspective is that it creates adversity and conflict, inside ourselves, and outside in the world around us. It reinforces the negative. When you can't get along with your neighbor because he mows his lawn at odd hours, and you dislike him for it and stop talking to him, you create conflict. When I can't have a spirited but civil dinner table conversation with a person of the other political party, I create conflict. When you spray pesticides on the little critters in the garden, you create conflict. When I forbid my children certain activities or certain behavior, it creates conflict.

How about looking at it the other way round, in the affirmative? This refocuses our outlook on what we *like*, on what we *want*, and want *more* of. How about rewarding your children (even just with kind words) for the type of behavior you would like to see *more* of? How about marching for peace? How about modeling the behavior you would like to see in others? How about making a list of all the things and people you do appreciate? How about remembering everything that went right today?

The war within and without keeps going if we keep feeding the fire. How about starving that fire, instead?

Lousy emotional reactions   September 5, 2014

"How other people react is their karma, how you react is yours," my yoga teacher said a while ago. When the supermarket cashier is grumpy, or the boutique salesperson is curt, I find it unpleasant and it makes me uncomfortable. When someone is angry I tend to take it personally and think the anger is directed at me. Most of us react that way. But it helps to put emotional reactions into perspective.

Imagine your boss just reprimanded you for submitting your report late. When you step out of that office you feel pretty lousy and might snap at the first person that comes along. Remember, though, the one who feels lousy is you, not your co-worker who happens to walk down the hallway. If you snap at your co-worker she probably thinks that she did something wrong, when instead something happened to you. See how intertwined we are?

It helps so much to be aware of our emotional reactions in order to diffuse them before they cause damage. How about taking a few deep breaths, going to the bathroom or the coffee station for a brief break, or being honest with your co-worker and saying, "My boss just chewed me out and I kind of feel lousy right now, do you want to have a cup of coffee with me?"

You can quickly and easily do a whole lot of damage with a crappy reaction, or you can choose to prevent a whole lot of damage by diffusing negative emotions.

Imaginary enemies   October 24, 2014

"You *make* enemies, they don't really exist," my wise thirteen-year old daughter said the other day while we were driving to the library. Did you nod your head just now, or did you think, "huh?" Here's the thing, at least from my perspective, our beliefs shape our reality, and our reality, at least to a large extent, shapes itself around our beliefs.

Suppose you feel really vulnerable and are fearful of someone breaking into your house. If this is a prevailing thought you play over and over in your mind, you may well be setting yourself up to experiencing just what you fear. When you understand the world around you as dangerous and adversarial, when you see people as "other" and treat them with mistrust because "well, you never know," when you believe you need to fight a cause or someone, you are making imaginary enemies. That is why some of our ways don't work so well, because we "fight" an illness, we "fight" pests and weeds, we "fight" obesity, and we "fight back."

Instead, let's cooperate, let's work together, let's try to understand, let's try to be compassionate—with others, with ourselves, with the environment. If you put out, with your thoughts, beliefs, and expectations, more of what you actually want to experience you will get more of that back.

They had a point in the sixties when they said to make love not war. Enemies are imaginary because we make them up in our mind.

Drop the hammer   March 20, 2015

As a young manager I used to be stern, demanding, and forceful because I thought that that conveyed authority. I still tend to say things twice in a row, with different words, when I want to get a point across. But I am beginning to learn that people get it even when I don't hit them over the head with a hammer.

As a matter of fact, we (and animals, too, by the way) get it even better when we formulate a request in the affirmative. How would you prefer to be corrected? "Stop yelling," or "I can hear you well?" I ask my daughter to use her "morning voice" when she speaks loudly at the breakfast table. She gets it.

I read that the universe doesn't understand the "not" part. We are similar, as are animals. We understand better what another person wants (and it sounds much nicer, too) if she says it in kind words, instead of reprimanding what she is critical of. Instead of, "Don't be late," why not try, "Please be on time, we begin at eight o'clock sharp?" Instead of, "Your table manners are terrible," try, "Fork in the left, knife in the right hand;" instead of "You forgot your homework again (grumble grumble)," try, "It makes my life a lot easier if you hand your homework in on time, and I can give you a better grade, too;" instead of, "Don't you scratch my couch," try, "Here is a great scratching post for you."

Deep listening   April 10, 2015

Deep anything is about doing whatever you are doing more thoughtfully, more mindfully, focused on the task, not thinking about either past or future. You can practice Deep Living, Deep Speaking, Deep Playing, or Deep Walking. It's like doing a meditation or mindfulness practice. Deep Listening is listening to your partner with an ear to her story, her needs, her feelings. When you listen to someone deeply you hear where she comes from, you open your heart to her, you respond to her needs.

Here an example of listening and responding shallowly:

You: "I just twisted my ankle."

Me: "Oh no. You know, that happened to me last winter, and I went to the doctor, and the doctor. . . .blah-blah-blah."

In this case I am not tuning into what you just said, instead following my own narrative. This is Shallow Listening, something we all do all the time.

Here an attempt at listening and responding deeply:

You: "I just twisted my ankle."

Me: "Oh no, that must have hurt. What happened? (pause to let you respond) Is there anything I can do for you?"

The difference is a shift from the *me*-perspective to the *we*-perspective. Deep Listening tunes one hundred percent into your partner. It really deepens relationships.

The best things in life are free September 4, 2015

Recognition, appreciation, love, comfort, understanding, respect—we all thrive on them. What's even better is that they are free. And as a gift they cost nothing. But the deal is this: you have to give first. After that, the more you give, the more you get. For some reason it doesn't work the other way around. You can wait a long time to get if you are unwilling to give first. It's all about opening up, putting yourself out there, going out on a limb, and then enjoying all that comes back.

And it's gratifying both ways, for the recipient as well as the receiver. That's why volunteering is so rewarding. Or gift giving. Or helping. Or praising your employee or student for a job well done. Do you know how good it feels when someone says to me, "How can I help?" That question in itself is a gift.

So give, give, and give some more. You may just like what comes back.

Face-to-face is best February 9, 2016

Phone conversations and go-to Meetings are one thing. Sure, they save time, money, and energy, and permit easy communication across long distances. Facetime, Skype, and other apps that permit you to see your communication partner are better. But nothing beats an actual face-to-face, whether in a business or private situation.

Real people, deep communication. There is simply no substitute for experiencing your partner's emotions, facial expressions, body language and, dare I say, vibes. We pick up so much information subconsciously from eye expressions, gestures, body language, and energetic qualities that simply gets lost otherwise.

Without face-to-face contact we easily misconstrue and misunderstand because we literally don't get the full picture. When we are together face-to-face we experience the whole person, seen and unseen aspects, and get the complete picture. Would you rather have dinner with a screen apparition of your friend or the real thing? There is a reason for business lunches and dinners, for meetings, for business travel. A virtual experience will never be the same as the real thing, and the cost savings may not always be worth it.

Say yes! March 11, 2016

"The secret of change is to focus all your energy not on fighting the old, but on building the new," Dan Millman's fictional counselor Socrates said in Millman's *Way of the Peaceful Warrior*. This is profound and cannot be said often enough—I must have written several blog posts along those lines, all saying the same thing in different words.

The universe doesn't hear the word "no," it leaves it out, it simply ignores it; so do animals, people, and especially young children. Guess what they do when you say, "Don't jump around on the couch." Guess what your cat does when you keep saying, with a look towards that couch, "Don't scratch that couch!" Guess what you do when the boss says, "Don't do it this way." You'd rather not listen because it doesn't feel good to be criticized. Besides, the boss didn't define how he actually wanted it done. But guess what you do when the boss says, "That report was written just the way I wanted it, thank you for a job well done." You listen, you acknowledge, and you do more of the same because you love being praised, and praise feels good.

So when it comes to anything, be it children's behavior, employee behavior, your own health, life, define clearly what you want, not want you *don't* want, and move in that direction. Move forward instead of looking backwards. That way you get more of what you want because the universe gets it.

The glue of relationships   March 24, 2017

Profit and trust are difficult to reconcile. It's easy to lose trust when money enters the picture, especially in the business world. When profit, our highest cultural value, reigns over trust, or compassion, or mutual benefit, it undermines a relationship. But trust is the glue of all good relationships. When we lose trust in someone because they value their company's or their own financial benefit over a cooperative and open relationship, we tend to tread backwards, withhold from ourselves, and close up. Business relationships often display a certain level of distrust or cautiousness because a business's ultimate goal, by definition, revolves around profit.

However, once we become aware of the tie-in between money and trust, it's possible to work for the mutual benefit of both parties by consciously working towards a win-win situation, a scenario that benefits both parties, or partners. Trust is the ultimate glue of any relationship. Build trust and you create a bond.

Good humor   March 31, 2017

You probably know that laughing is good for your health and well-being. I love good, gentle humor—especially the kind that is self-deprecating—because it's not done at someone else's expense. Dressing someone down in order to elevate yourself: "Look at that garish dress, haha," creates a win-lose situation. When you humor yourself on the other hand: "Oh dear, hopefully stepping into that dog pile will bring me a whole bunch of good luck," nobody else gets emotionally hurt because you pointed out the irony in something you yourself did; then everyone can laugh freely and without guilt. It's a win–win.

Because I'm a bit serious by nature I have always admired people who can humor themselves, who don't take themselves too seriously. But as I'm maturing I'm getting a little better at it, more easily in writing, when I have some time to think about what to say, although I will never be a stand-up comic.

Self-deprecating humor doesn't offend anyone but the humorist, so it's safe and harmless. I heard someone say that it only works well if you're confident already. Then it can be put to good use—as a speaker to loosen up an audience, as a teacher to lighten the classroom atmosphere, as a boss in a meeting. Self-deprecation makes us human and approachable. How is your sense of humor?

Okay to admit   *May 5, 2017*

Why do people have such a hard time admitting they've made a mistake? We are all humans, we all make mistakes, we regret many of them later. But, geez, say so. I won't think less of you, on the contrary.

I find it especially important in my role as a parent to acknowledge a mistake and apologize for it—yes, to my child. Otherwise I am modeling behavior I don't want to see perpetuated. We have this underlying cultural belief that we are perceived as weak when we say, "I was wrong," "I made a mistake," "I'm sorry," or "I wished I'd never done this." I build up a huffing and puffing resistance and fight response to a lame, "Wasn't me" or "I would never have done this." When, on the other hand, someone says right away "Oops, so sorry, my mistake," that feeling implodes and my reaction softens immediately.

How cool would it be if a politician or CEO honestly said, "I made the wrong decision at the time, but I understand the issue better now and take full responsibility, and I promise to correct the situation." Wouldn't you appreciate the humanness in that person? I guess this behavior all starts with you and me, though.

It's not about you!   June 13, 2017

When you become annoyed at your friend for saying something not so nice about your outfit, it's *not* about you, it's about *her*. You obviously liked your outfit when you got dressed this morning. But your friend has different taste and likes different styles, or colors, or outfits. When she reacted to your outfit it had to do with *her* ideas, *her* taste, *her* likes—not *you*. We get it all wrong when we believe others criticize us for *us*.

You have no control over many of the things that happen to you during the course of the day, whether it's people's comments, their demands, or unexpected events. What we *do* have complete control over (at least in theory until we get used to this new way of thinking) are our emotions and feelings, our *own* reactions to our interactions with life.

So, you became miffed at your friend. Well, who knows why she said what she said. But you'll never know until you make an effort to find out and dig deeper. You might consider saying something like, "Sounds like you don't like my dress." And your friend might completely surprise you by replying, "Oh, I've always hated the color red," or "That dress reminds me of something my mother used to wear, and it brought back a lot of negative memories." You never know where someone else's comments are coming from until you tune in and actually ask. Then there is true connection and you'll find out that it was about her all along—*not you.*

Changing my world   June 30, 2017

When I change my perspective the world around me changes and adjusts. Amazing.

Here is how it works. During a recent introduction to NVC—nonviolent or compassionate communication—we were supposed to recall a recent incident that irked us, and look at it from two perspectives, our own, and then the one from the other person. I recalled my daughter's recent phone call from school, in the middle of the morning, that she didn't feel well and needed to be picked up. I noticed that I felt annoyed, irritated, and resentful for being interrupted during work—my needs were for space and independence. However, once I turned the perspective around and understood that she felt miserable, hurting, and anxious, and that she needed affection, compassion, and nurturing, all I wanted to do was come to her rescue and comfort her.

It took my own inner shift, not coercion, not anybody else's action or change in attitude, to want to help her. Amazing.

Reflections on
cultural change

Organic epiphany   May 11, 2012

I had this epiphany a while ago when I needed to buy a new duvet cover and saw an organic cotton one on sale. Previously, I had mostly thought about organics in terms of the health benefits to my family and myself—that buying and eating organic foods would prevent us from ingesting pesticides, harmful additives, antibiotics and growth hormones, genetically modified and weakened foods in general. But the perspective is much more encompassing, which is why I ended up buying the organic cotton duvet cover.

With this purchase I voted for a healthier environment and a healthier agriculture, because that cotton didn't get sprayed with pesticides or subjected to chemical fertilizer. I also voted against the industries that develop and manufacture these fertilizers and toxins. I voted for the health of the farm workers who weren't subjected to the poisons, and lastly I voted against genetically modified crops and the big conglomerates that develop them.

To weed or not to weed   June 5, 2012

Weeds are not "bad" per se, after all they are part of the biodiversity of the plant kingdom. It is more a matter of perspective how we see them. Out of a *laissez-faire* attitude I have weeded relatively little in both our vegetable garden as well as the rest of the garden this year, and I am finding that the whole garden is just so filled with all kinds of plants, more so it seems than in other years. Our bees are happy, wild flowers and herbs are spreading, vegetables are self-seeding from one year to the next—it's incredibly abundant.

Some "weeds" are actually edible, such as dandelions or purslane, for example. Other "weeds," which we call wild flowers, are pretty in the garden, or beautiful in a vase, gathered in big generous bunches. Others yet spread an incredible scent, as does our wild and wildly growing honey suckle. Making weeds my allies, instead of "fighting" them as enemies, is a much more cooperative approach, as The Healthy Environment Group and Bill Finch explained recently in separate write-ups.

Are you a Cultural Creative? October 15, 2012

It is quite possible that you have never heard of them. It is also quite possible that you are one of them, or us. It is estimated that we—yes, I am definitely one of them—are more than eighty million strong in this country alone, and that there are about two hundred fifty million of us worldwide. The funny thing about the Cultural Creatives is that they don't realize how many others share their values. Cultural Creatives believe in authenticity, in quality over quantity, in contributing to a healthy planet, in transparency, in many of the values that people embrace who are into sustainable and green living, homesteading, the farm-to-table and locavore movements, sustainable agriculture, and so forth. The Occupy Wall Street Movement is full of Cultural Creatives, but fizzled because of lack of leadership and lack of realization of how many actually share these new values.

Dare I call it a newly emerging consciousness structure? If this has perked your interest, you can find out more about The Cultural Creatives, and whether you are one of them, on Paul Ray and Sherry Anderson's website. They are the sociologist/ psychologist husband-and-wife team who gave this emerging phenomenon its name and wrote a book about it in 2000, while filmmaker Frigyes Fogel made a movie about the movement, its ideas and values, and is now planning a TV station.

The busy trap November 27, 2012

Being busy for the sake of being busy—Tim Kreider wrote in the *Times* recently how we worship busyness as a virtue and are addicted to it. It fills life with meaningless activity, and I have caught myself at it. Checking Facebook or email five times a day, snacking, driving around shopping, hovering over the children, staying late at the office because of peer pressure (because working hard is a virtue here in America, right?), even when the day's work is done.

Busyness is not only a mechanism of procrastination, but also a shield against delving deeper into life in general, filling emptiness with busyness. I say, "work smart" not "hard," and fill the rest of your time with meaning. It's quality that counts, not quantity.

Black Wednesday?   November 28, 2012

Ever since our evolution away from a nomadic lifestyle to a life in permanent settlements we have lived out the economic misconception of scarcity, believing that there is not enough to go around, and that only "the fittest survive." Among many other apparitions, this cultural delusion is responsible for the Black Friday—and now Black Thursday—phenomenon. Instead of spending meaningful and quality time with family and friends, many now rush out of the house even before Thanksgiving Day is over, to stand in line, fight the crowds, and feed the big box stores some more money, truly believing that there won't be another deal around, that "it's now or never."

We vote with our spending dollars. How about voting instead for local merchants who add diversity, creativity, and a sense of community to our lives—and enjoying your turkey dinner a little longer, too? Otherwise we'll have Black Wednesday soon.

Crazy times, creative times   December 21, 2012

Crazy times here on Earth! Between the end of the Mayan calendar, the insane Sandy Hook shooting last week, and all the other serious problems we have created—environmental, cultural, nutritionally, agriculturally—it is a pretty chaotic world.

But it is also an insanely creative and opportune time to awaken and turn things around (before it truly is too late). Like in a huge thunderstorm, where warm and cold air masses collide, the old and new are colliding in front of our eyes. There are so many conservative and fundamentalist movements out there, composed of people afraid of change, confused by what is going on, and who would like to take refuge in the old known ways.

And then there are the new movements, from the Occupy Movement, to the Arab Spring, to the many women's lib initiatives all over the world. Because 12/21/2012 and the end of the Mayan calendar usher in a new consciousness, 2013, more than any other new year in recent times, is a grand opportunity to follow your heart, make sweeping changes in your life, make a difference in the world, in your community, and for yourself. Move this evolving consciousness along in the direction of a better world, a more cooperative world, a more compassionate world, a more creative world, a saner, and healthier world.

No man is an island   June 25, 2013

I just finished reading Emily Matchar's book *Homeward Bound* on the New Domesticity movement. The book is about women (and some men) embracing home and hearth in a new cultural twist, about being tired of corporate pressure and the lack of the government's and the corporate world's response to women's (and men's) family needs here in this country, while European countries are introducing more and more of it (more guaranteed daycare spots, more maternity and paternity leave, more vacation time). This movement also comprises the so-called "preppers," who believe in taking things into their own hands in light of a perceived potential Armageddon that the government, they believe, is not prepared to manage, and become as self-sufficient as possible. Some of that self-sufficiency drive is shining through in homesteaders who only trust the safety of their own vegetables, the quality of their own childcare and school instruction (note that this lone-man-on-the-frontier and homesteading syndrome seems specific to this country because of its pioneering history).

In Nature everything is intricately interconnected in the famous web Chief Seattle (supposedly) spoke about ("whatever you do the web you do to yourself"). When you remove elements of a system (eco or social), like removing a card from the middle of a house of cards, the system starts to crumble. Since we are part of Nature we also exist within an intricate web of relationships and associations. By the way, the more meaningful our relationships are, the richer our lives. People with a large social network and strong relationships live longer.

When we opt out of the web some part of the web crumbles and weakens, and what we are able to accomplish diminishes. Matchar makes this crucial point. When people become so self-centered, as in If-public-education-crumbles-I'll-just-pay-for-private-school,   or If-the-general-food-supply-is-unsafe-I'll-just-grow-my-own, or If-corporations-don't-give-a-damn-about family-life-I'll -just-quit, then we have a problem. Then the country no longer pushes towards a common agenda that benefits all. You may call me a socialist, but what is bad about jointly rooting for the highest good for all (as opposed to my own highest good)? What is bad about making education accessible to all, and thereby increasing the level of intelligence and critical thinking of the entire population? What is bad about pressuring the government to put proper food safety measures in place? It benefits all of us in the end. We need to remain within the web and help to improve the entire web instead of jumping ship and going it alone.

"Ask not what this country can do for you, but what you can do for your country," as one famous president said not so long ago.

Why fair trade?   July 18, 2013

Have you read about the awful recent garment factory collapse stories in Bangladesh? Do you know what fair trade coffee or fair trade bananas are? Well, here it is. According to Elizabeth Henderson, an organic farmer for thirty years, who helped organize the Domestic Fair Trade Association, "A fair price is the right price with a triple bottom line people-profit-earth."

Fair Trade began with such crops as bananas, coffee, and cocoa from South America because the local farmers were being exploited in the interest of a low sale price and the biggest possible profit for Dole, Chiquita, Chock-Full-O'Nuts, or whoever else. The idea of Fair Trade is a facet of the "new economics," the newly arising cultural paradigm of watching out for all of us, not just some of us—the health of the farm worker, a fair wage for the farm worker, a sustainable agriculture that does not harm the Earth, a healthy product for the consumer, and a fair profit for the banana exporter/importer or cocoa powder maker.

Fair Trade is a win–win situation, all involved parties involved profit; non fair trade is win-lose, because only one side wins. Of course this means that the end product costs a bit more. But what's wrong with that if in the end we all profit from it?

The DFTA (Domestic Fair Trade Association) now promotes the same principles of health, justice, and sustainability on a domestic level. And, to complete my loop to the recent garment factory disasters, through all our awakening to these issues the beautiful win–win principles of Fair Trade will surely make a leap to the garment factories abroad so those workers can work in safe buildings and work for fair wages.

Why men need women   July 22, 2013

Women are more generous than men, Adam Grant noted in his *Times* article of the same title yesterday. Yesterday, too, a friend raved about her daughter's female boss, who provides her with benefits and vacation time even though the daughter only works part-time. I am not saying that all women make better bosses. But we are naturally more nurturing and empathetic, while men are more driven and result oriented, the yin and yang of Chinese philosophy.

Yet, we shouldn't want to do away with the guys in business. Balance is everything, and we need both energies—the driving and the nurturing. The article reports that women inspire the men in their lives to greater philanthropy and generosity (i.e., Melinda Gates is the driving force behind the Bill and Melinda Gates Philanthropic Foundation, according to Grant).

I believe that the incoming cultural paradigm is, or will be, more balanced, more heart based, more sustainable, because we are beginning to realize that strict bottom line, capitalistic, exploitative yang behavior is dangerous to our health, environmental and otherwise, because it is unbalanced. We need both energies, since they complement each other perfectly.

Women are slowly leading men away from yang domination to greater balance. The rise of women's empowerment, their greater involvement in business and politics, and their slow and steady recognition as equals attests to that. Adam Grant concludes his article with the (wise) recommendation for men to follow our lead.

The Great Transformation   October 11, 2013

Hold on to your seats . . .then go with the flow. The Germans are calling it "Die Große Veränderung," "The Great Transformation." The shift is here, the consciousness shift (the Mayan calendar ending 2012 et al.) that is driven by climate change. Or we could say that climate change (which we created) is now accelerating our consciousness shift. Oh well, they all inform each other reciprocally anyhow.

It is the Great Transformation to a cooperative, peer-to-peer (as Jeremy Rifkin, the economist, writer, public speaker, and consultant to the German government, says), lateral (no more from-the-top-down) culture and consciousness structure that will radically transform our approach to energy and its distribution, and with it to our culture at large. And, Rifkin states, it will all happen within one generation! (If we don't get off carbon within thirty years, he says, we are doomed. We better go with the flow, and fast, than resist, because otherwise it'll be even more painful).

I do want to scare you a bit out of your slumber, as Rifkin did at this past weekend's conference on Sustainable Living at the Omega Institute, when he said about climate change that we are really not being told the seriousness and urgency of the issue here in the U.S.—Germany, Denmark, as well as Costa Rica, are on the forefront of all things climate and energy change. Rifkin says about climate change, "It's terrifying!"

So this consciousness transformation, that my book *Deep Living* and this blog are about, albeit from a slightly different twist (they are more about returning to a more balanced heart and spirit based way of living as a basis for healing from the inside out), is actually forcing itself on us from the environmental side. And from there it will transform our economy from the bottom up, and with it our entire culture. Out with scarcity based economics, in with an economy of abundance (see also Charles Eisenstein's *Sacred Economics*). In importance this shift is bigger than the Fall of the Roman Empire, and it will happen faster and reverberate around the entire globe.

Cultural change, here it comes! The thing is, if you are an active participant it's an exciting opportunity to help create a new cultural paradigm; if you resist it (or even deny that climate change is happening) you will be dragged kicking and screaming along in the wave of change. You choose—creative opportunity and empowerment versus victimization. We live during such a crucial, a bit scary (why is change scary?), yet such an incredibly momentous, period in the history of humanity, let's make the most of it!

No Me Generation   December 2, 2013

Turns out that *Generation Y* is very different from the *Me Generation*, the baby boomers. *Generation Y*, those born after 1980, is more into the quality of life and less into financial success—quality over quantity. "Meaning" and "making a difference" are terms that come up. Meaningfulness for these millennials is associated with "other orientation" as well as giving, as opposed to egocentrism and personal gain. The term *ecocentrism*, as in ecosystem and in contrast to egocentrism, has also been used for those who think "green," who care about doing what's good for all and Nature, versus what's just good for you. This is a real shift and in sync with the shift or rise in consciousness we have been told is underway. These convictions will have huge implications on our culture and politics.

Fasten your seat belts! Move to the side boomers!

On happiness   January 21, 2014

"Happiness comes from your perspective," says Marianne Williamson. A recent study showed, to the astonishment of the researchers, that depressed people were depressed because they had negative thoughts, not that they had negative thoughts because they were depressed. This goes to show that you can train yourself to think more positive thoughts in order to change your outlook on life.

But your government's priorities sure help. One country that has made happiness its national business is Bhutan. Bhutan has created the Gross National Happiness Index and studies how happy its people are, and what can be done to improve the situation of those who are not. Bhutan's search for happiness is not a recent endeavor since its 1729 legal code already stated, "If the Government cannot create happiness for its people, there is no purpose for the Government to exist." What a country!

And Denmark was crowned the world's happiest country in the 2013 World Happiness Report (not sure why Bhutan does not appear in the report), figuring at the top with the other Scandinavian countries, the Netherlands, and Canada. Social support, gender equality, a culture of generosity, freedom to make life choices, good life expectancy, lack of corruption at the leadership level, and a large GDP all contribute to making for a happy country. Priorities, priorities!

Happy Earth Day   April 22, 2014

Today, I am wishing you a "happy" Earth Day, with the caveat that our worldwide window to tackle climate change is beginning to close—few days ago I read something like fifteen years. If we don't achieve a definite downward curve on carbon emissions within that time frame our lives will change drastically, and not for the better. We can't keep shrugging our shoulders and putting the onus on "the government," because "the government" gets its nudge from all of us. Things change when true pressure is exerted on "the government" from all of us. Change comes from within, moves from the bottom up and out, and government is a reflection of us.

The onus for drastic change is on each one of us! Now! Don't throw your arms up in despair at the enormity of our challenges. Instead, make a conscious effort to embrace what needs to be done by fully accepting our environmental calamity and committing to make a difference.

So, what can you do? Here are lots of ideas, and the more of them you incorporate into your life the better for all of us. Recycle and compost your kitchen scraps; plant a garden; buy an energy efficient vehicle (or at least consolidate your trips, or car pool); insulate your home to the max and consider installing new tight windows; read all you can about climate change and the environment in general; buy local; bring your own bags to the supermarket (no more plastic bags! there are several gigantic plastic swirls in the Pacific Ocean, the size of some states, and plastic does not, I repeat, *does not*, disintegrate for hundreds of years); drink well water and forego buying water in plastic bottles (and who knows what leaches into that water from the plastic anyhow); read all you can about industrial food production, then make a drastic change to what you buy to feed your family; install solar panels on your home (interesting tax incentives, leasing, and the panels get cheaper and cheaper); consider a geothermal heating/air-conditioning system (after tax credits, cost is similar to a conventional system and you'll be off fossil fuels); switch your electric supplier to one who provides one hundred percent electric from renewable sources; eat less meat (it's better for you anyway); spread the word to other people and inspire them to make a difference; most of all—inform yourself and become aware.

Don't be surprised that none of this is for free. However, you have a choice of making these investments *now*, on your own terms (consider them an insurance premium for environmental health), or shortly being forced by environmental circumstances into a very ugly reality that money and technology will no longer be able to improve.

If you love your planet make it a happy Earth Day by making a difference for yourself and your children and grandchildren.

Pizza every night?   July 28, 2014

How boring. I'd rather eat something different every night. And from all over the world, too. We are so fortunate nowadays to have access to such a great selection of foods. We are exposed to so much diversity. Japanese sushi, Moroccan tagine, French snails, Middle Eastern mezze, downhome hamburgers, Italian pasta, Russian borscht, and on and on. . . .

For that same reason—enjoying diversity—traveling is so eye-opening because we get to see how other people live (and eat, and think). We need to get out of the house to learn to expand our vision because we learn through comparison. Comparison and juxtaposition show us alternatives, options, different ways of doing things. Only when we know what our options are can we begin to choose. Homogenization—a Walmart or Starbucks on every corner no matter how far from home we go, or pizza every night, or the same religion for all—makes us culturally poor and life dull.

But with diversity we must learn tolerance. You don't have to have sushi, but it's great that it's available for those who like it. Let's enjoy the possibilities and excitement that diversity affords us instead of hitting those with different opinions or preferences over the head. As Frederic the Great said, "*Jeder soll nach seiner Façon seelig werden,*" or, "Each must live as he sees fit."

From Me-age to We-age   October 3, 2014

What an amazing time we live in! Big cultural changes are happening as we speak, although it's sometimes a bit difficult to see them when you're in it. From a greater perspective it's been said that we are entering the Age of Aquarius, and that our consciousness is evolving from the me-age to the we-age as we proceed deeper into the new millennium. Climate change is now forcing the issue and mandates that we unite across the globe to mitigate and address this biggest of current problems.

Culturally, there are already a lot of indications of a shift from the me-age to the we-age, and it's all been jumpstarted by the internet. While spiritual people have always said that we are not separate, that it just seems that way, the internet now demonstrates directly how connected we all are—and this is nothing woo-woo. Think of how the internet has changed our lives in the past two decades. "Knowledge is power," they always say, and that is what the web has brought us with all this shared information right at our fingertips. It has led to so much more transparency and accountability, which empowers us all. Whether Wikipedia, free music sharing, free movie and eBook sharing (and yes, there are royalty issues involved that go way beyond the scope of this post), free college lectures, free internet help forums on anything and everything, it's all there for the sharing and using.

On the service side there is the Uber car service, and several spin-offs, that circumvent the traditional taxi and car service net and lets riders contract directly with car owners for their transportation needs. The lodging site Airbnb circumvents the traditional hotel industry and lets homeowners share their homes directly with tourists for a fee.

Connecting empowers us.

A better world?   November 7, 2014

Are you happy with the current state of affairs? If the answer is *yes* read no further. If the answer is *no*, please keep reading. Have you ever pondered how things got to where they're at? Do you believe it's the politicians' fault? Or the corporations' fault? Or everyone else's? Maybe you're not sure.

We like to blame because we don't really like to be responsible. It's easy that way. We're off the hook. However, that perpetuates the status quo. Change can only happen if we do something. Remember what Kennedy said so famously, "My fellow Americans, ask not what your country can do for you, ask what you can do for your country." If you are tired of your old job do something in order to find a new one. Get your resume together, put the word out, research potential companies, and, most importantly, formulate what this new job is supposed to look like. *What do you want?* If you put "wishy-washy" out there, "wishy-washy" will come back. Imagining what your perfect job looks like in detail, and then focusing on only those companies that are suitable, will get you much better results than simply complaining that you don't like your job.

So it is with the rest of life. You have more power than you think. But you have to do something to effect change. And you have to imagine what exactly you want.

There's hope yet   February 27, 2015

Watching the mainstream news you might just tear your hair out over the current state of affairs of the world, what with climate change, ISIS, the state of our environment, and all those civilization diseases that afflict us. Enough to become depressed. Mainstream media knows what sells, and it's blood, gore, and fear mongering. Things look gloomy from that perspective, indeed. I don't disagree that our world is in major disarray—environmentally, economically, and culturally.

But there is hope on the horizon and I am optimistic. Here is why. I see all those new, holistically oriented, grassroots movements bubbling up here and there and everywhere. Barbara Kingsolver already stated in 2007, in her wonderful book *Animal, Vegetable, Miracle*, that these kinds of holistic pockets are no longer limited to the two coasts, but are popping up all over the country.

Between the green living movement, the slow food movement and all its related efforts and awareness initiatives, climate activism, so many many environmental efforts, the localization movement, homesteading and the new farm movement, waste reduction, composting, and recycling efforts, alternative and homeschooling, cooperative living, alternative healing modalities, and then some, a cauldron full of new energy and ideas is bubbling.

Other than perhaps the tiny nascent environmental movement there was none of this when I arrived in this country in the early 1980s. This development has burst into the open on all fronts in just a quarter century. Amazing! When you know where to look it is so exciting and encouraging! Be a part of it.

Playing in heartland   May 8, 2015

When I play, which I don't do often enough (although I consider some of my cooking time play time), I am truly in the moment. Young children play all the time. That's what they do. It's their job. They learn by osmosis, through playful imitation of the adult world. Playing leaves the left side of the brain, the rational–analytical side, out of the equation, and stays in right brain mode. Play is creativity and spontaneity, not calculated analysis. Games like chess or poker, or truly competitive sports, are not play because they are about left brain strategy, which involves thinking in words.

What makes play "play" is its state of mindfulness, which is absent of words. The younger children are, the more they exist in this state, not thinking about what they ate for breakfast, or what they will play this afternoon. Martha Beck wrote in *Finding Your Way in a Wild New World*, "The way to cope with the increasing complexity of the wild new world is to play more." Her enlightened advice for dropping into the mindful world of play is to leave the words out—by the way, that's exactly where meditation is headed. "Words are the language of the mind, emotions are the language of the heart," a fellow grad schooler said to me in that regard. Drop the words, drop your beingness down, down, down—until you reach your heart. Here words don't exist.

Words separate, words tag, they have their role, but we spend most of our time in word land and not enough in heartland. Let's go on a journey to heartland and play.

Salutogenesis   September 15, 2015

It's a term I hadn't heard until I read an article this morning on approaches for dealing with the refugee crisis in Europe of all things, and coined by medical sociologist Aaron Antonovsky. Without ever having heard it called *salutogenesis*, I embrace this model in my thinking, in this blog, and in my book *Deep Living*. It is, after all, about strengthening what is healthy instead of destroying or treating what's diseased. With regard to healing the body the idea is to strengthen the immune system and support the body's ability to continuously regenerate and heal itself through a deep mind–body relationship. Why? Because stress, negative beliefs, and emotional problems are responsible for eighty-five percent of our health problems, as has been estimated. Salutogenesis is a proactive, preventative, and positive approach, while our mainstream Western model, in very broad strokes, is about fixing, eliminating, destroying, cutting out, or band-aiding what's diseased.

Translated to my deep living approach, salutogenesis is about standing for, and promoting more, of what we want (healthy and rich soil, clean air and water, honesty and transparency, dignity for all people, sufficient food for all, and on and on), instead of ranting and raving about what we don't want (pollution, corruption, disease, poverty, refugee crisis, and so on).

Do you like your glass half full or half empty? It's all about turning our attention to the positive aspect of things.

Simply amazing   March 16, 2016

It's an amazing time we live in. Things are developing so fast, changing at lightning speed, and so much information has become available in the past few decades, with the advent of the internet, that it's just mind boggling. I love the internet.

My Encyclopedia Britannica set from 1966 is collecting dust and taking up bookshelf space (although filled bookshelves look nice, and people think you're smart when you have lots of books). My parents are holding on to, and still use, three sets of encyclopedias (one from the early 20th century, one from the mid-20th century, and one from the end of the last century). An encyclopedia is what you needed way back when— but no longer.

Knowledge is power, as they say, and the internet has exponentially increased the availability of information in an incredibly short amount of time. Everything and everyone gets reviewed and evaluated. You can read reviews and you can write reviews. The power lies in the two-way street. Bad products, bad restaurants, bad schools, bad doctors, bad professors and teachers can no longer hide, and good ones are rewarded quickly.

Doctors are no longer the sole keepers of medical information. Instead they have become your co-treaters in the healing process as the internet has empowered us with information on symptoms, treatment methods, options and alternatives. Amazing!

Universities post free online lectures and courses, and free education is available in many different forms and formats. Encyclopedias have become obsolete, as the latest information on anything is available and updated in real time at the touch of your smart phone, anytime and anywhere. Amazing!

Living in the countryside I used to have limited access to many food items and other products. No longer. You can buy practically anything over the internet and have it shipped practically anywhere—and it comes fast. Amazing!

With increasing visual content on the internet how-to information is now available in the form of videos—how to make an eggplant parm, how to lay tile or install carpet, how to make a birdhouse or apply make-up, how to block annoying callers on your particular phone model, anything and everything. Amazing!

Let's be amazed and grateful and awed.

Shhhhh
June 3, 2016

We lived right by the road for over twenty years, and didn't realize how much all that background noise affected us—until we moved. Now we live in a very quiet place, and it is heavenly peaceful all the time.

The machine age is only about one hundred and fifty years old. Before that the world was quiet. Imagine for a moment a world without engines—no cars, no airplanes, no kitchen machines and appliances, no noisy farm equipment. With the development of electric cars we may actually be heading back in that direction, as my husband noted the other day. Have you sat in an electric car? You can't even hear that the engine is running. Generating electricity from solar panels is completely silent as well. I remember the roar of the furnace in our old house when the thermostat switched it on, the geothermal system in our new place is almost noiseless.

Quietness is grounding and reboots your mind. Are we headed back to a quieter world? Will it help us to become more grounded and less frazzled? When our children were small we reminded them every once in a while that they needed to stop chattering for a bit, and said, "It's quiet time now."

Find some quiet time every once in a while, it brings peacefulness.

Why we need elders   June 14, 2016

Children and grandchildren used to live either with, or in proximity of, their parents and grandparents, and in traditional societies still do, giving the younger generations access to older people they can trust, and who can guide them because they've "been there, done that." Nowadays we don't always have access to that elder wisdom because parents and grandparents often live far away, or perhaps we have excluded them from our lives for various reasons.

But we all need mentors, guides, counselors, and people who help us navigate our complex world that is going through huge changes. The world is changing faster than ever. Often the grandparent generation, even if around, is not keeping up with technology and social changes, and is thus unable to help because they may feel lost themselves. Heck, parents are often lost, and their teens flounder and resort to drugs, alcohol, and the virtual screen world because they lack emotional support and wise guidance. Between climate change, environmental calamities, changing economic paradigms and social structures, the refugee crisis from the Middle East and Africa, and violence and terrorism seemingly popping up anywhere and everywhere, we have a lot to chew on.

We need very special elders to guide us through these intense times so we don't get lost in despair, anguish, or aloofness. They are around, I know some of them. Intergenerational communication is more important than ever.

Social transformation how-to   October 7, 2016

Do you take for granted how our culture does things and thinks about things? In other cultures things are done differently. Thirty-eight countries worldwide have banned the cultivation of genetically modified crops, while the U.S. has not. The U.S. is the only Western country with capital punishment. Do you wonder? Are you curious why values differ from one country to the next? Maybe you have wondered about the process of changing such fundamental beliefs?

Believe it or not, it boils down to this: it all begins with you. Change usually does not trickle down to us mere mortals because the government changes its policies in anticipation of your desires. The other way 'round: the government changes its policies because of pressure from somewhere, whether consumers and voters, organizations, lobbyists, or corporate donors. Whoever screams loudest and longest gets heard. It's a critical mass thing.

When you want change, the first thing to do is to look at your own actions and beliefs to make sure they are aligned with the change you wish to see. Create the change in your mind and see how affiliations around you will shift. The organic movement for example has grown exponentially in the past twenty years because individual food awareness has grown within so many of us. That's why such change is called grassroots. It begins at the bottom and grows up and unfolds from there. Fracking was banned in New York State in 2014 because of such from-the-bottom-up momentum. What is your vision?

The new values   December 13, 2016

A few years ago we hired a bright young man who left our company after only three short months. He decided that he didn't want to work as much, and proposed to work less hours for less pay (which didn't work for us).

There is a new set of values around, and it's quality-of-life-based. The younger generation, of which many did not vote in this past election because they did not feel heard, has a different set of values from the twentieth century ideals of a profit-based, fast-paced, career-track oriented hustle for the next promotion and bigger salary. The new values are not about chasing the next buck, but about a better quality of life, sustainability, trust and transparency, as well as sharing, cooperation, and creating community.

We get a glimpse of these new values in the many grassroots movements that are popping up everywhere: deeper awareness about food issues (such as veganism, reduction of food waste by way of redistribution, organics, the local food movement); increasing awareness of social values (fair trade movement, raising the minimum wage, shorter work hours); the many environmental organizations, whether awareness raising or preserving land for future generations; transparency (such as promoted by Wiki Leaks) and pricing information available on the internet; free sharing of music, education, and information on the web. Skills and things are shared and swapped without the exchange of money, in hour exchanges, seed exchanges, repair cafés, tool libraries, cooperatives of all kinds, clothing and book swaps, and via Freecycle. Some communities are experimenting with local currencies, some employers with job sharing, flextime, paternity leave, summer hours, and more time off.

In an earlier blog post I introduced the *Cultural Creatives*, the name Ray and Anderson gave to people like myself, and many who share these values. Know that these impulses are glimpses of a new cultural-economic model breaking through from underneath. It's incredibly exciting to know we are part of something bigger, and that we are experiencing this shift to new values in real time.

Money co-ops   March 15, 2017

If there were a credit union in my town I'd transfer my money in a minute. The difference between a credit union and a bank is that banks are for-profit. That means that the more fees they charge and the less interest they give the wealthier they become. Credit unions, on the other hand, are non-profit organizations working for and on behalf of their members. In a way a credit union is something like a banking co-operative. In general their fees are lower than banks' fees, their interest rates tend to be slightly higher, their executive salaries are lower, they have fewer branches, and they are more locally oriented. Their purpose is to work with and for *you*, as opposed to for their own self-preservation.

With social changes and tendencies towards more cooperation and more transparency, credit unions are becoming more and more popular because their practices are more customer oriented. It is millennials that are driving the credit union growth trend, and credit unions are growing faster than other financial institutions.

Do you have a credit union in your town?

No waste   *March 28, 2017*

Nature leaves no waste, only people do. Nature's waste is sustainable because its decomposition follows a sustainable cycle in which every part feeds the next step in the cycle endlessly. Animal waste and dead plant material compost back into the soil, carrion eating birds and little critters take care of animal carcasses, trees absorb the carbon dioxide that animals and humans exhale. It is only us humans who have devised production processes that transform natural materials into stuff that is either itself not recyclable (think plastics) and creates trash that way, or whose manufacturing produces side effects in the form of waste and pollution (any industrial process).

Worldwide many towns and cities strive to become zero-waste by 2020. The goal of zero-waste is to recycle and compost everything so nothing goes into the landfill. It takes a strong commitment from the city, and a persistent education effort, to overcome people's initial resistance and learning curve. Take a look at your household trash and recycling logistics. Can you do better?

Since Nature leaves no waste let's remember that we, actually, are Nature, too.

A better world   June 20, 2017

It seems that many things in this world are currently a mess—the environment in general, the way we treat each other, social issues, climate change and erratic weather patterns, our medical paradigm and quandary, our food supply, our politics—oh, my!

But I truly believe that there is a better world under all this chaos. We just need to create it, envision it, and imagine it. How do you do that? You have to imagine it, then you have to live it—that's what Gandhi said. There is indeed a lot of beauty already on this planet; there are a lot of wonderful, kind, compassionate people on this Earth; the healthy food movement is growing stronger every day and we have all the inspirational models already out there; climate science shows what we need to do; we know that we want people to thrive, feel safe and secure, have easy access to good medical care and good education; and we know in our hearts that there are better ways of communication than judging, belittling, condemning, surmising, and berating.

Instead of condemning and fighting and criticizing what you don't want, just put yourself on the side you prefer—every day—with your words, your dollars, your thoughts and beliefs, and your world will change for the better.

Unlimited energy   July 7, 2017

And by this I don't mean your personal level of energy, I mean energy to produce electricity for transportation, machinery, and electronics as a basis for our economy.

Rob Hopkins founded his *Transition Movement* in England in

2005 based on the idea that we are coming to the end of the fossil-fuel era and need to revert to local economies to reduce our reliance on oil. One element of this reasoning, the suggested need to decrease our energy requirements, is now changing. While the local economies movement is stronger than ever, it is for different reasons than the potential lack of energy.

We are now seeing a strong movement towards renewable energies, much of it based on solar and hydrogen, but also wind, geothermal, and others. My prediction is that we will actually have way more energy than we have available now, an overabundance of energy, and that geopolitical alliances will shift because everybody, not just a few nations, will have access to enough energy. We will never ever run out of sunlight and hydrogen. So even if a country didn't have enough sunshine, well, nobody will ever run out of hydrogen. Iceland is such an example that is already energy independent and produces all of its energy from hydro and geothermal sources.

Volvo, no longer Swedish but long owned by the Chinese, bets on the future of electric cars, and is throwing their Chinese power and money behind it. Hydrogen is unlimited and may become one of our foremost energy sources in the form of hydrogen fuel cells.

Meanwhile the return to local economies, away from globalization, will remain a strong movement because people want agency, they want responsibility for, and involvement in, their local politics, be it for reasons of local customs and culture, sustainability, land use, or general policies. But the return to village life will no longer happen due to a lack of energy.

Health and wellness thoughts

Forever young   May 16, 2012

The world shapes itself around your beliefs. Positive beliefs empower you, negative beliefs, on the other hand, hold you back. Whether you believe you are starting to "become old" when you notice a little ailment here or there, or whether you consider it simply a passing appearance that will self-regulate back to perfect health, is based in no small part on your beliefs. Whether you are an old or a young thirty, an old or a young ninety, has so much to do with your beliefs about life, the body, aging, sickness and health, and your attitude in general.

Harvard psychologist Ellen Langer staged a famous experiment with nursing home residents, who were brought to live for a few weeks in an environment that emulated a period several decades earlier. Well lo and behold, their minds literally turned their bodies' physical clock backward in small but significant ways (read more about this amazing study in her book *Counter Clockwise*).

Some beautiful examples of older inspired and inspiring people have come across my Facebook page. They remind me that your attitude and beliefs can keep you forever young until the day you die. One of them is the ninety-four-year-old yoga master Tao Porchon-Lynch; another one who brings a smile on my face every time is an older piano- playing couple; and the last one is the former Rockette Louise Neistat, who tap-danced until her recent death at ninety-two.

Two more well-known examples of the power of the mind are world records (it is not unusual for several more people to break a world record as soon as someone has broken one) and the supposed difficulty in conceiving children (couples who have resigned themselves to adopting a child oftentimes conceive as soon as they have actually adopted).

Love those germs   September 12, 2012

Enough fighting already! We fight too much—enemies, wars, illnesses, and death. They are all simply another aspect of the same thing. Balance, not eradication, is the answer.

A little dirt, a little dust, a healthy amount of bacteria, are all actually good for you. Most of us know by now about the drawbacks of antibiotics—those indiscriminate bacteria killers prescribed much too liberally to humans and animals over the past decades in an effort to kill all the "bad" bacteria. *An Epidemic of Absence*, on the possible relationship between our modern germ killing frenzy and the surge in recent civilization and autoimmune diseases, possibly even autism, was published recently.

So eat your yoghurt, sauerkraut, kimchi, and pickles (naturally fermented, not the supermarket kind with vinegar), drink your kefir, kombucha, wine, beer, or mead, and clean your home and body with gentle and natural cleaning and cleansing products instead of those germ-killing antibacterial soaps and cleaners.

Health is a balancing act   November 20, 2012

Healing is much more than "fighting" symptoms with mechanical or chemical means in order to get rid of them. Health is an ongoing balancing act that requires continual and never ending internal adjustment.

When you are in tune with your body you begin to notice even slight imbalances, such as fatigue, digestive system upsets, aches, or stress. Such minor imbalances can easily be rebalanced with gentle methods, like rest, better food, lifestyle adjustments, or energy healing methods (EFT, acupuncture, homeopathy, and others).

Healing is about recognizing your needs. When your emotional and physical needs are met your body, mind, and spirit all function in harmony and unison, and you are healthy as a consequence. When, on the other hand, you have unmet emotional needs, and you keep ignoring them and your body's nudging messages, more serious physical symptoms are eventually bound to develop over time from this stress.

"Perfect health" is fleeting and unattainable on a continuous basis, healing is ongoing as long as you live.

CAM   May 17, 2013

CAM is short for "complementary and alternative medicine" and covers all healing modalities other than the Western allopathic model, or "conventional" medicine. Western allopathic medicine is based on a mechanistic model of the human body, in which the different body parts can be treated by specialists and independently from one another (e.g., the heart by a cardiologist, the kidneys by a nephrologist, the feet by a podiatrist, the mind by a psychologist or psychiatrist). Diagnosis is based on detailed examination of all visible parts of the physical body. Treatments are geared towards eliminating or reducing symptoms; they are not geared towards healing the root cause of the matter, because that is not part of the belief system.

Treatments range from cutting out diseased tissue, to injecting or administering substances that reverse the symptoms (but also usually have side effects, undesirable for the most part). This is similar to bringing your car in for a check-up and having its oil and windshield wiper fluid checked and refilled, the tire pressure verified, and the spark plugs exchanged.

This model is successful in emergency medicine (accidents, broken limbs) and for acute illnesses, where no time is to be lost to save a life. It is not so effective for afflictions that have a connection with the psyche (most of them) —did you ever consider that heart disease might have to do with matters of the heart (not the organ, but the emotional heart)? Here, the model of one-standard-treatment-cures-all does not always work, as we can see from the varying successes of treating cancer, heart disease, psychological and psychiatric disorders, diabetes, auto-immune diseases, and on and on.

CAM works with a different model of the body. In this model the body is more than a sum of its physical parts, it is a mind-body–spirit entity that exists in an energetic universe. Some examples of CAM modalities are homeopathy, healing with herbs, acupuncture, reiki, Ayurveda, but also massage therapy, music therapy, yoga and meditation. These methods all help to rebalance the underlying energy system of the body. It has been said that about eighty-five percent of all illnesses are due to emotional imbalances, which means that the underlying emotional blockages or psychological conflicts need to be resolved to dissolve the physical symptom without reoccurrence. It has already been acknowledged that lifestyle changes can do wonders—regular meditation reduces stress, a better diet and more exercise give you more energy, and less stress and more harmony in life are beneficial in general. That's all spiritual stuff. There is definitely more to our bodies than what we can see.

Pill or self-heal, the power of beliefs   May 28, 2013

We used to believe, truly believe, that the Earth is flat and that we would fall over the edge if we went too close. We also believed, truly believed, that our planet was at the center of the universe. Heck, we even burnt someone at the stake for saying otherwise.

We believe other things now, but they are as firmly embedded in our minds as those from earlier times we now call silly. One of them concerns self-healing. We currently don't really believe that we can self-heal, or let's say that we only believe it under certain circumstances (which makes no sense; it either works, or it doesn't). Usually we quickly run for outside help—doctors, pills, tests, and so forth. But think about this: When you have a cold and eat chicken soup, or drink tea, to feel better, you don't believe that the chicken soup or tea actually heals the cold. You understand that you, your body, heals the cold, and the tea or soup simply help. When you break a leg and get a cast you don't actually believe that the cast is what heals the bone, you understand that you/your body heals the bone, and the cast simply keeps the limb from moving to aid the body in the healing process. Under those circumstances we all actually agree that we self-heal and that tea, chicken soup, and cast are aids or props.

But the belief system is shaky because we still need an outside "expert" with "expert" methods to help us heal more "serious" ailments. When we take pills or resort to various treatments, we believe all of a sudden that they actually caused the healing. Yet, when the treatment doesn't work so well, as is often the case, then we are at a loss—but we wouldn't doubt or adjust our belief system.

You may have heard of voodoo deaths, whereby someone actually ends up dying from a combination of their own fear and the combined energy of the village community that does the condemning. You may have read about the study on placebo knee surgery for arthritic patients that ended up treating the cause without actual surgery (!). The fact is—our beliefs are enormously powerful! And when we don't heal, it is often because negative beliefs, or residual trauma, are in the way and counteract the process (there are of course exceptions, such as afflictions we are born with). When the negative beliefs get cleared, the body can heal itself. Check out the recent book *Use Your Body to Heal Your Mind* by psychologist Henry Grayson to explore this subject further.

Healing is shifting   *August 2, 2013*

"Doctors don't dispense wellness, they suppress symptoms," Dr. George Wootan, a pretty enlightened family practitioner in West Shokan, New York, said recently during a talk I attended. There you have my gripe with allopathy, the Western medical healing paradigm. Suppressing symptoms is not healing because it maintains the same underlying emotional and thought patterns.

A friend recently posted something like this on Facebook, "Has it ever happened to you that all of a sudden you see something in a totally different light, and you wonder how it happened, and why you did not see it in that light all along?" A shift has happened. Some of these shifts happen gradually over the years, some of them happen suddenly. Eckhart Tolle describes such a sudden shift in his first book *The Power of Now*. After years of dread and depression he woke up one morning and suddenly the world looked bright and beautiful to him.

True healing comes from within. It arises out of shifts in thinking, in consciousness. I believe that almost all ailments are due to emotional hang-ups—such as negative thoughts and beliefs, emotional trauma, or past life residues. When you clear these, through your own work and intent, or with someone's help, the energy channels open up and the shift happens, all by itself.

Feeding the body and the soul   September 20, 2013

I am currently—sort of (on and off)—doing Deva Premal and Miten's twenty-one-day mantra journey. During the introduction to Day 5, Miten points out that, just as we feed the body (with food obviously, but perhaps also with exercise and fresh air), we also need to feed the soul, that other part of us. We can feed our soul in all sorts of ways. I think anything that emphasizes the quality of life feeds the soul, such as beauty, friendship, love, or serenity (did you notice that these are all things money can't buy?).

Mantra chanting, as Miten explained, is one such soul food. The German September 2013 issue of *GEO* had a small article on the benefits of singing together. Researchers discovered that the hearts of a group of mantra singers beat in synchronicity. The controlled breathing of mantra chanting, similar to the controlled breathing practiced in yoga, slows the heartbeat down and strengthens it, which is so beneficial. When a group chants mantras together each individual melds into the group togetherness through the common synchronized heartbeat. Neat!

Cause and effect in healing   January 14, 2014

A headache is a cause of something deeper in your psyche, as is for example stress, low self-esteem, depression, or any number of symptoms we may experience. These symptoms have causes (try to analyze what happened before the onset of the headache— too little sleep? stress? overwhelmed?).

Allopathy, as the Western healing system is called, treats the effect, the symptom your body puts out to signal that something is not right. It does not heal the cause! A medication is a chemical that alters your body chemistry by sheer force (and with more or less harmful side effects) without changing the cause of headache, or depression, or whatever. In the same way, surgery, for example, removes the effect by force without addressing the cause. This type of treatment does not always work predictably (which is worth a whole other discussion).

Energy and alternative healing modalities, such as reiki, acupuncture, homeopathy, and so forth gently realign your internal energy stream by removing blockages. Once realigned you can feel what it is like not to have the symptom—*ahh*. These methods are gentle and have no harmful side effects. However, even they may still not heal you on a soul level unless you shift the beliefs or thoughts that created your imbalance in the first place. So, here too, the symptom may reappear in its former or another form.

The ultimate healing mechanism is awareness on a consciousness level of what created the symptom, and then dissolving or shifting that belief. While this is a simplified outline of the healing process, and there are also other causes of illnesses, it has been estimated that eighty-five percent of all afflictions are due to emotional issues.

Are accidents really accidents? March 7, 2014

Someone in my larger circle of acquaintances hated her job and "needed a break." Guess what happened next? She broke her ankle and was out on surgery, in a wheel chair, then physical therapy. She really got her break.

So are accidents really "accidents"? Do they rain down from the sky, haphazardly, to the unlucky, or is there more to it? I realize that some people may be hard-pressed to take full responsibility for what is happening to them and consider the possibility that they create their own experiences. My pet peeve is the lawsuit against McDonald's a while back, when the company was sued by someone who suffered burns from spilling hot coffee all over herself. Was it really McDonald's fault, because the coffee was too hot? Or was the woman perhaps clumsy or distracted? So much in our culture is a reaction to avoid taking responsibility.

Henry Grayson, the psychologist who recently wrote *Use Your Body to Heal Your Mind*, recommends inspecting what an affliction (this word is more encompassing than "illness") either prevents you from doing or permits you to experience. In the case of my acquaintance. the ankle break permitted her to take needed time off from work. A cold, flu, or stomach bug gives your body and mind time to rest (remember—of all the people exposed to the same virus, not all get that flu or stomach bug—mm: Why is that?). Also consider that any affliction lavishes you with other peoples' compassion, kind words, and care—something we all love to experience, and some people sadly might perhaps *only* experience when they are sick.

What about other kinds of accidents? Some accidents may prevent you from driving for several weeks, some may prevent you from using your hand for a while. These consequences may have particular meaning to you, if you ponder your circumstances. Or they may not, and might be karmic. In the end we all have to come up with our own answers to these kinds of deep and big questions, and those answers are usually very personal. But they are worthwhile pondering.

How's your memory?   May 2, 2014

A few days ago I attended a seminar on memory improvement. Two interesting points, in common with holistic living, came up.

The first one was presented in the context of techniques for remembering names when meeting new people. Matthew Goerke, the speaker and an expert on memory development, explained what meditation teachers are always stressing, that the untrained mind is like a wild horse. It goes wherever it wants to—not necessarily where you or I want it to go. Without intent and focus, a person's name basically goes into one ear and out your other because your mind is meanwhile chattering about your to-do list for the afternoon, or that you'd really like a tuna fish sandwich for lunch. Key is to take control of your mind, to be in the *here and now*, to tune into the person you are meeting, to repeat her name with focus and intent while shaking hands. Chances are you'll remember her name again when your paths cross in the supermarket aisle, instead of remembering the face vaguely but neither perhaps where you met or her name.

The other point had to do with the beliefs we subconsciously hold about ourselves, and how, in this case, they impact your memory. You might say or think, "I have a hard time remembering things," or "My memory is getting worse the older I get." This type of running internal commentary is like a mantra and becomes a self-fulfilling prophecy if repeated often enough. Instead, begin to repeat how you'd actually like to be, even if you have to fake it before you truly believe it (our minds can't distinguish between the two, so "fake it 'til you make it" is good advice). Better to keep saying to yourself and others, "I have great memory," or "My memory is getting better every day." If you repeat it often enough this, too, becomes a self-fulfilling prophecy.

No need for ginkgo biloba. Instead, be mindful and focused (tell your mind where you want it, keep the reins tight), and think and speak what you *do* want (a great memory in this case), not what you *don't* want or fear (such as "I keep forgetting things," or "I can never remember names"). When Matthew Goerke asked us at the seminar, "How's your memory?" we learned that our answer should be, "Great."

Rest is best   June 10, 2014

. . .or about getting to know your body. It is invaluable to listen to and understand your body, to learn to read its signals. While it is easy to pop a pill and not give a symptom a second thought, it is helpful and eye opening to look at symptoms as an expression of something that is going on in your mind. After all, body and mind are inextricably linked.

A headache is something that can oftentimes easily be deciphered as lack of rest, or a subconscious issue that bothers you, or a looming decision that's got you in a tizzy, or something stressful going on. Popping that headache pill will eliminate the symptom, at least temporarily, but it will not solve the actual problem. So it makes sense to tune in and go a little deeper to try to understand what caused the headache.

A pulled muscle's cause is easy to identify, and the treatment is straightforward. But, again, popping that pill helps to cover the pain, while it does nothing for actually giving the muscle the rest it needs to heal. Besides, why did you pull it? No time to warm up? Impatience? The answer may be to slow down. And the pulled muscle does that for you. When something is not quite right in my diet, my stomach makes itself known right away. Whether too much meat or carbs, not enough greens, too much sweet stuff—my stomach tells me. Stress, too, shows up in my stomach.

Two questions to ask yourself about a symptom are, "What does this symptom prevent me from doing?" and "What does this symptom force me to do?" Breaking a leg prevents you from running around, having a cold makes you rest, losing your voice forces you to be quiet. There can be a lot of symbolism between a symptom and your particular need at this point in time. Open up to it. By suppressing the underlying emotional or physical need your body will show you in a different way what it needs. So—tune in.

No to TV   July 25, 2014

We have no television, never have, never will. Although it's nice to save a few dollars on cable, that's not why. And don't get me wrong, we love good movies and do watch them. I'm really talking about a totally different reason for not having television, the one that Waldorf schools have advocated all along.

Television, with its massive amounts of manipulative commercials that constantly disrupt programs and the stream of thought, and with all those pictures of ugly events from natural disasters to man-made ones, creates a distorted and highly negative picture of the world. Weather predictions, too, are designed to create hype. Think of the nervous anticipation the weather people create before a winter storm or a heat wave (and sometimes nothing much manifests, and you could have spared yourself all that adrenaline). When, on top of that, you hear the same story repeated over and over, over the course of a day, or two, or three, the nervy effect is cumulative and highly toxic.

Not only does it feed our anxiety level, another consequence is our heightened need for safety and security to compensate for this seemingly dangerous world. Think of it, teachers wish the kids a "safe summer" before summer vacation. When friends go traveling, we wish them a "safe trip." And we hover over our children, taking opportunities away from them to grow and become independent by letting them assess risks on their own. Remember when you were young? I bet you were more independent than your own children are now.

Call me old-fashioned, but I prefer by far my paper news. I can skim over the ugly stuff, filter it, or read it without that frenetic, anxious energy of live on-screen reporting. Without television the energy in our home is a lot more peaceful.

On balancing   October 7, 2014

"If you don't take care of life, it becomes messy," my yoga teacher said this morning. Health is an ongoing and continuous balancing act that requires that we keep checking in with ourselves.

Health is not "just there," it's something that needs to be worked at. And health consists both of mental and physical aspects. Not only do we have to eat healthy foods, and get enough sleep and exercise here and there, we also need to dust off the cobwebs in our mind on a regular basis. For that we need time to check in with ourselves.

Whether that means meditating, journaling, simply being aware of what goes on "up there" or in your body, doing yoga, or any other practice that rebalances and refocuses you doesn't matter much. It just matters whether you do it or not. Otherwise it's easy for things to get out of kilter, and that's when we can get sick, either physically or mentally.

Take a look at your life and scan it for such balancing activities. It is good to spend time alone with yourself. Such a grounding and alone practice could also be writing a poem, doing calligraphy or ikebana (the Japanese art of flower arranging), gardening, or going for a massage. The possibilities are endless as long we do such activities in a mindful way that focuses inwards.

If you don't already have such an activity in your life consider making time for one, or two, or three.

Please don't take my sunshine away   October 14, 2014

The whole controversy about sunscreen and skin cancer has made us scared to be out in the sun without a thick layer of white sunscreen on our face, long sleeves, and a hat. However, this prevents us from soaking up vitamin D through the skin, which the body needs for calcium absorption and a healthy immune system. So we put ourselves between a rock and a hard place and take vitamin D supplements (and make the whole supplement industry very profitable along the way), although those supplements are not the same as sunshine *au naturel*. In addition, we need at least ten minutes of real sunshine per day to reset our circadian rhythms, which promote a healthy sleep cycle.

And, talking about the absence of sunshine in our life, people have gotten so used to wearing sunglasses for fashion looks that their eyes are becoming overly sensitive (have you ever seen an indigenous person with sun glasses?), when in reality our eyes were made for sunshine (other than extremely bright conditions, such as a walk in the Sahara, skiing in the mountains under a sunny sky, or a sunshine filled glacier walk).

Get some real sunshine by going out at lunchtime, parking your car a bit further on a sunny day and walking that extra half mile, sitting on a park bench and soaking up the sun, getting off the subway or the bus one stop ahead, and doing a bit of hiking and biking on the weekend.

Ebola's mystery   November 11, 2014

"One boy dies, another lives." This was a headline in yesterday's *Times*. But is it Ebola that is mysterious? Is the flu mysterious? Some people get the flu, some don't, and some even die of it. So it goes with all afflictions. Maybe the mystery lies elsewhere, although it is typical of our present culture to see the mystery in Ebola, in the flu, and in any event outside of ourselves. But every person is unique, everyone comes with a different agenda or predisposition into this life, everyone deals with situations differently, everyone lives in unique and individual surroundings.

We seek predictability from science, we want the same test results validated again and again to "prove" something scientifically. We want to believe that a certain treatment will result in the same repeatable healing mechanism. But it doesn't! Our immune systems are unique, our mental patterns are personalized, our healing mechanisms are different from one person to the next. Instead of trying to shoehorn the effects of treatments into supposedly predictable outcomes, which they don't, how about looking at healing as a personal and individual process that is unique to each one of us?

I believe that the mystery lies in our human nature, not in Ebola.

A new medical paradigm   March 31, 2015

What if it weren't necessarily the microorganism that made us sick, but that healing depended instead on the condition and resilience of our own immune system, our constitution, our circumstances, and how our body handles strains to our well-being?

Liise-Anne Pirofski, infectious disease specialist at Albert Einstein College of Medicine, clarifies that a particular microorganism can harm one person and leave another unharmed. Too often, Dr. Pirofski says, we simply try to combat a certain microorganism with antibiotics or vaccines. Yet we have not found vaccines against tuberculosis, malaria, herpes, or fungal diseases. Instead, Dr. Pirofski suggests researching how to strengthen the host.

In essence, Dr. Pirofski proposes a radical paradigm change, away from the pathogen-as-culprit and towards understanding instead how to strengthen and heal the person. This goes against the grain of the Western medical paradigm that treats the perceived pathogen, and is more in line with the thinking of CAM, complementary and alternative medicine, that treats the whole person.

Ask not what makes you sick but how you can heal.

The next healing frontier   July 24, 2015

The five eras of healing, as presented in *The Healing Code* by Drs. Alexander Loyd and Ben Johnson, are an eye-opening way to look at the history of medicine and healing and where we currently stand.

According to the authors, the five historical stages we have gone through are praying and the belief in healing, herbal remedies, pharmaceutical/chemical remedies, surgery, and, now, energy healing. It is thought-provoking to look at healing from that perspective, as we are beginning to realize the limitations of both surgery and pharmaceuticals, our most recent eras, although both can of course do wonders in critical and acute conditions. When surgery is used for the removal of a malignant condition, removal doesn't always seem to get to the bottom of a condition and it may return, e.g., tumors. Pharmaceuticals have side effects, often debilitating, e.g., chemotherapy, and suppress or displace symptoms without healing the underlying condition. Moreover, pharmaceuticals can't seem to heal chronic conditions, merely keeping them in check.

Energy medicine, on the other hand, besides having no side effects and healing gently (no invasive procedures, no cutting), can dissolve underlying emotional knots, conditions and trauma which have manifested in physical symptoms, dissolving those along the way. Mainstream medicine will of course resist this low tech approach as very little money is to be made compared to the billions that now flow into the medical and pharmaceutical industries. The fact that we call them industries is a problem in itself. How about calling alternative healing modalities healing arts instead?

Let food be thy medicine   August 14, 2015

A lot of food bashing has been going on in recent years about the Western diet, and rightfully so. While many cultures have been using foods to heal the body through their various properties (as do Chinese or Ayurvedic medicine, for example), over here we have been eating food that actually makes us sick, foods that promote cancer, diabetes, arthritis, food allergies, heart disease, and what not. Those sick foods have been euphemistically labeled the Western Diet. But what if foods could actually heal, as Hippocrates was already arguing in ancient Greece? "Let food be thy medicine, and medicine be thy food." Eating properly actually keeps us healthy and full of energy, or supports the healing process by boosting our immune system, if we have healing to do.

Seems that many of us have to relearn what healthy foods are. Healthy foods are not processed (if it has more than one ingredient, and comes in a package or can, it's processed) and are as fresh and local as you can get them (more life energy), have not been sprayed with toxins (yuck, who wants those accumulating in their body?), have been grown in healthy and rich soil that has been fertilized as naturally as possible (otherwise, where are the minerals and trace elements supposed to come from?), includes meat that comes from grass-fed animals (corn makes cows and their meat sick) and dairy as well, which should also be unpasteurized, unhomogenized, and raw. And make green and red your favorite colors. Leafy green vegetables have been labeled a superfoods because they have such a concentration of vitamins, minerals, and trace elements (more so than fruit!) and are high in fiber and low in calories and carbs, while the reds are loaded with antioxidants and phytochemicals.

And lots of raw (no, I'm not an advocate of a raw food diet) is especially good for you (do green smoothies if you don't like to eat your greenies raw—blend an avocado, leafy greens (stems and all), lemon juice, an apple or a carrot for slight sweetness—*voilà*, the healthiest breakfast prepared in minutes (and believe me, it makes you feel full and satisfied).

Diet, exercise, and well-being   September 30, 2015

For a while there it seems that Coca-Cola had us duped into believing that exercise, more than diet, is the most important factor for weight loss and well-being. The Coca- Cola Company gave almost three million dollars to the American Academy of Pediatrics over the past three years, as the *New York Times* reported yesterday in a spill-it-all article. In addition, Coca-Cola infiltrated many small community organizations with their web of donations and sponsorships, and "bought" dieticians and scientists. Talk about covert and not-so covert manipulation and unscientific science.

The bottom line is this: diet is tantamount to a healthy body, more so than exercise. You cannot make up for poor food and drink choices by exercising more. It is much more important to clean up your diet, learn to shop and cook, and make healthy food and drink choices. Once you've got that down pat, exercise is a complementary health component, keeping in mind that every body—and everybody—thrives on a different type of exercise, and on different weekly amounts. A gentle and automatic weight adjustment, and an increase in energy and well-being, naturally follow a switch to a wholesome diet.

Fidgeting is good for you   January 6, 2016

I am not a very sporting person, but because of all the noise about the importance of exercise, I've done some reading on the necessity of movement. Our bodies are made to move in gravity, and the much-touted stand-up desk is not the cat's meow either if you stand still at it all the time.

Our current computer-based work culture condemns us to sit for long hours, yet our bodies thrive on perpetual motion. Point in case—when your body aches, you need to move more, not less. As a matter of fact, as little as walking briskly half an hour each day increases your life span, supposedly, by about seven years. The message of our overcompensating workout culture is to exercise vigorously at the gym. But that is not necessarily the best answer, unless of course you just love it and thrive on it—everybody has a different need for type and intensity of movement. Just don't sit for long hours without getting up and stretching often (long commutes are a killer). Kids fidget and want to move naturally. Yet we force them earlier and earlier to sit still. Fidgeting is the body's natural way to signal its need for movement.

We contract out lawn mowing, house cleaning, and house maintenance work, yet these all make for excellent exercise. You don't need an expensive gym membership to move your body. Joan Vernikos, who studied the effects of zero gravity on the body for NASA, concludes in her book *Sitting Kills,* "Standing up often is what matters, not how long you remain standing," at least thirty-two times a day, she recommends. It is our interaction with gravity that's so important. The main message about movement is, "continuously and gently," not "seldom and intensely."

Good dental diet   April 15, 2016

A few days ago, when I went for my biannual cleaning, the dental hygienist noticed that I had a lot less plaque than the last time around. Lo and behold, we'd changed our diet quite a bit since then, cutting out almost all sugars, refined carbs, all starchy and sweet vegetables, as well as most grains, and eating a lot more vegetables in general.

In the 1930s dentist Weston Price studied the relationship between dental health and the diet of indigenous people versus people from industrialized countries. His famous study linked deformed arches and crooked teeth, as well as poor general immunity, to poor diet, not only in Western people but also in the younger indigenous generation whose parents had adopted more Western types of foods.

Nowadays we are quite aware of the effect of sugar on teeth, but Price also pointed deeper, to vitamin and mineral deficiencies in food due to poor soil conditions—already then. From our present perspective, almost a century later, with processed foods having crowded out whole and plant-based foods even more from our diet, and from knowing that our soils are yet more minerally deficient, the picture looks even worse. When I was a kid, it was quite rare for children to get braces; now it seems ubiquitous.

The message is clear—cut out the sugar, increase your veggies, and opt for organics if you can, since organic foods have a considerably higher mineral and vitamin content. The Weston Price study shows that your grandchildren will thank you for it.

Getting out of your groove   April 19, 2016

It's easy to get into a groove, into routines that are comfortable but perhaps no longer serve a purpose, trotting along on autopilot. Multilingual people, and those who keep up intellectual work throughout their later years, are less likely to get dementia or Alzheimer's, as has been shown. Our minds operate like an old-fashioned record player that digs deeper and deeper grooves into an old vinyl record. Thus, over time, it becomes more difficult to change routines, see things afresh, learn new stuff, and remain flexible as a reed in the wind.

Once aware of this we can remind ourselves to change around how we do routine things, which helps the brain to build new synapses and remain adaptable. When I set the dinner table, I often deliberately switch around the sequence and direction in which I place the table settings, starting at a different chair, or beginning with glasses instead of plates. Or I'll take a different route going shopping, left around the mountain instead of right around the mountain. Other ideas might be to change the sequence in which you brush your teeth (using your left hand for a change), wearing a color you otherwise would not, or taking the day off to celebrate just because.

Any other ideas?

Spring cleaning   May 6, 2016

Spring cleaning is not only a good idea for your house. By all means, wipe off those spider webs, clear out your closets, wash your windows, and get rid of stuff you no longer need. But spring cleaning is also good for body and mind.

To help it transition into spring, you may choose to do a juice cleanse for a day or two this time of year. Lemon water with a bit of maple syrup, or vegetable juices, are recommended, in addition to lots of water and herbal teas. I am just getting over a cold, and those happen more in the spring and fall as the body's way to clean itself out—although I can't say that that cold was by design.

And finally, after house and body, the mind needs dusting as well. Yesterday we did a helpful meditation in yoga in which you observe your thoughts (those that keep popping up when you try to meditate) and tag them to try to find a pattern, and then amend it over time. Categories might include "judgment," "feeling," "negative belief," "positive observation," or perhaps "planning." Most of my thoughts were of the last category, meaning I kept pulling myself into planning and anticipation mode about future events. On the other hand I was happy to discover that no negative thoughts kept floating by. The message I got from the meditation was, "Be in the here and now."

What message will you get?

Slooow yoga   *May 10, 2016*

Slow anything is beneficial as an antidote to our fast-paced lives, whether Slow Food, Slow Yoga, or Slow Something Else.

Slowing an activity delves deeper because there is more time to be attentive and reflective, and experience what you are doing more deeply. I go to both Slow/Gentle Yoga and Yin Yoga classes, and they are wildly different from the yang-oriented vinyasa, power yoga, or hot yoga practices that are currently so popular as an extension of the frenetic gym culture. In Yin Yoga, which is floor-based, poses are held for longer periods of time, usually three to five minutes, and up to ten. The connective tissues have time to relax and stretch, encouraging energy flow and releasing blockages. Slow or Gentle Yoga, as its name indicates, takes it slowly and gently, and can be compared to a moving meditation. Breath is important in this practice. Both are calming, and I usually come back feeling like I've had a spa session.

You can slow any activity to experience a different spin on things. Try Slow Cooking, Slow Eating, Slow Teeth Brushing, Slow Showering, or Slow Reading.

Holistic healing   June 21, 2016

About two months ago we were surprised to find a nickel-sized open wound on our cat's upper neck. It looked raw and nasty. We remembered that we had felt small scabs in that spot earlier. The holistic vet told us to put some coconut oil on the wound for a few days and see. It didn't improve, so I took the cat to the regular vet. He prescribed an antibiotic, a cat collar, and antibiotic ointment. The cat collar was a disaster for our poor cat; she hit herself everywhere, couldn't reach her bowl and eat properly, and became dejected after two days. The collar came off, and the holistic vet paid a house visit for laser treatments on the wound, reiki, and acupuncture. The wound was still the same, but our cat ate well again and became her usual self, although she diligently kept scratching the wound open, and licked off the antibiotic ointment as best she could.

I am no longer so impressed with the Western healing model. It is useful and even life-saving in many instances, but powerless in many others. Often, therefore, either a combination of Western and alternative methods, or an alternative approach altogether, work better. But finding the appropriate treatment method can be like navigating a dark hallway at night and tapping the wall to try to locate the light switch.

I decided it was time to speak to the cat directly to get her take on the situation—unlike humans, animals are amazingly aware of their own condition. We contacted our local animal whisperer, whose help we had previously enlisted. It seemed that the broad-spectrum antibiotic had not eradicated the particular bacterium that had lodged under the cat's skin and affected her nerves after a simple scratch wound. This made the wound feel deeply itchy and hot. The cat whisperer recommended mixing three homeopathic remedies, one in particular for nerve damage, in water, and dripping a drop on the wound several times daily. The results were still not convincing, because our poor cat still scratched when the cold water drop hit the wound, and after another two weeks I heeded our holistic vet's further recommendation to try noni lotion, made from the Hawaiian noni fruit, which is antibacterial, full of healing antioxidants, and inoffensive when licked and ingested. Finally, success!

It has been a long and very winding, road, but the wound is almost healed. In the end we will never know what caused the turnaround, whether any one remedy did the job, a combination of several, and whether our persistent intent played a role.

Too acidic? October 21, 2016

Our body chemistry is healthiest at a pH of about 7.3, slightly alkaline. If it becomes too acidic, we become ill (when my daughter was diagnosed with diabetes 1, her body pH was at 6.8). Over-acidification makes us prone to cancer (tumors feed on sugar, and sugar acidifies the body chemistry), diabetes, heart disease, and all inflammatory conditions (over-acidification causes inflammation).

The mainstream Western diet is too high in acidifying, and too low in alkalizing, foods, and it's easy to become imbalanced. So let food be thy medicine to stay healthy or heal yourself—low tech, low cost. Food comes in all colors of the pH spectrum—it is simply a matter of awareness to eat more of the beneficial ones. In broad strokes, the foods that acidify the body chemistry are sugar (as a culture we are literally addicted to sugar and meat!), meat (the redder, the more acidifying), and refined carbs (as they transform immediately into sugar). Ha—you'll say. Exactly.

The foods that alkalize our body chemistry are most fruits and vegetables (not potatoes, and not bananas, as they are both highly starchy—starch also turns immediately into sugar). The most alkalizing vegetables are all the greens. Since we thrive with a slightly alkaline chemistry, we need to not only balance acidifying and alkalizing foods, but eat slightly more alkalizing than acidifying foods—hence the recent push for a more plant-based diet.

Of course each person is unique, and you need to test for yourself which foods work better for you and which don't. Some people are okay with breads and cheeses, others not so much. Some people are okay with reasonable amounts of pastured meats, others less so. Your digestive system and constitution are unique, and also tied to your geo-cultural and genetic heritage.

The main message is to increase the amount of vegetables (you've heard that one before), especially the greenies, cut out the sugar (no news, really), and drastically reduce your meat (go meatless every few days, switch to fish, do poultry instead of red meat or pork) and refined carb intake (less bread, pizza, pasta, waffles, bagels, and baked goods). Instead, increase the amounts of healthy fats, nuts, and legumes in your diet to meet your long-term energy needs (sugar is a false energy booster without nutritional value).

Hahaha   January 10, 2017

Laughing is good for you. As a matter of fact laughter should be prescribed as medicine. It reduces stress hormones, diffuses anger, triggers endorphins (those feel-good hormones), oxygenates and massages your organs, makes you feel relaxed, aids in the elimination of toxins, and boosts your immune system. That sounds like therapy to me.

Laughter is so good for you that an Indian internist, Dr. Madan Kataria, invented laughter yoga two decades ago.

The Mayo Clinic promotes laughter for stress management purposes, and it's an excellent addition to cancer therapy because a positive outlook improves your chances for healing.

A few years ago I tried out laughter yoga when a session was offered in my area. At first it seems quite bizarre to laugh with a bunch of people you don't know, about nothing in particular, and do a bunch of things to get everyone to start laughing for the simple sake of getting you to laugh. But soon enough it becomes contagious, and everyone in the room goes from giggles, to laughing, to full belly laugh in no time. Soon enough you don't know anymore why you're laughing, because you're not laughing at a joke or something someone did, but simply because everyone else laughs so hard. It's very cathartic and very funny and feels very good.

When was the last time you had a really good belly laugh?

A Ford or a BMW?   April 4, 2017

You get the difference between a Ford and a BMW. The BMW is a better car because the components are made of superior materials, the lengthy thought and testing that went into the design of the mechanics assure it will last long, and the driving experience is exceptional.

When it comes to food we have the same choices, between the Fords and the BMWs of foods so to speak, but. . . the choices you make matter a whole lot more than which car you drive. And I am not talking about caviar versus pasta. I am talking about *how* a food is grown or made, what goes *into* it, *how* natural it is—its inherent quality. Food goes *inside* your body; it literally becomes you. It gives you the energy to live, promotes building and healing the cells in your body, contributes to a good immune system, feeds the brain so you can "think on your feet," and insures your overall good health. My mother believes that she would have been taller if she hadn't eaten inferior food during the first six crucial years of her life, the six years of World War II.

Inferior foods, whether out of a carton and enhanced with chemicals, grown with pesticides, pre-made and over-sugared, fed antibiotics and growth hormones, or kept and slaughtered under horrific conditions, cannot give you BMW-quality health. The consequences can be manifold. Eating inferior foods can cause you to be more susceptible to illness in general because your body doesn't get adequate nutrition, you may tire more easily, have a troubled digestive tract, duller skin, less zest for life, think more fuzzily, become afflicted by chronic conditions, and even die younger.

Of all the Western industrialized countries, ours spends the least amount of money on food in proportion to average income. For the sake of your health, increase your food budget. You don't need a BMW to get around, but you need superior food to live a long, healthy, and beautiful life.

Infinite healing   May 23, 2017

Nature has an amazing ability to heal and regenerate. Two years ago I received a beautiful mini cyclamen. Somehow, after many months, it faded away until it had only one leaf left. It looked so sad.

I don't throw plants away unless they are completely dead, and I was determined to nurse this cyclamen back to its original health and vitality. I observed it every day, I made sure it was well watered and fertilized, and I watched for signs of new life. Lo and behold, a second leaf emerged after a while, then a third. Then one of our cats chewed the second leaf, and I felt discouraged. But my cyclamen now has six big new leaves and several new shoots. I am positive that it will make a complete recovery and produce beautiful flowers soon again.

Remember, *you* are Nature, too. *Your* body's ability to heal is just as infinite. Just look up Anita Moorjani's story of coming back from what the doctors thought was a hopeless state.

Crystal bowl healing   June 6, 2017

Last year I wrote about the theory behind sound and gong baths, because I was intrigued by the idea—as a holistic adventurer I gobble up all alternative therapies and love to try them out. In the meantime, I have finally been part of a crystal bowl healing session.

The sound therapist had laid out a rug in the large studio where the session took place. Crystal bowls of various sizes (different sizes for different sounds, some quite large) and various colors (I don't think color makes a difference) were set up on the rug, and wooden mallets were set aside for producing the sounds.

After a long, guided winding-down period, or *savasana* (my daughter coined the term *slowvasana*), we were all deeply relaxed and receptive. It had been suggested that we come up with an intent, because the deep relaxation coupled with the healing frequencies channel the message of the intent more easily into the subconscious, which guides—hold your breath—ninety-five percent of what we do—yes, indeed! Then the sound therapist began to produce sounds by rubbing along the edges of the different bowls. There is no melody or pattern to the sounds, so the mind has no place to cling to; it can drift and let go. Not only my ears, but my entire body, experienced the sounds—I felt with my body that sound is frequency. The deeper sounds of the bigger bowls were so powerful that the sounds filled the entire room and my entire body. Some sounds sent shivers down my spine, others appeared to travel from one side of the body to the other.

I ended up in a timeless space where the sound bath could have gone on forever; it was profoundly grounding and calming—definitely to be repeated.

Your beautiful microbiome   June 23, 2017

All the fauna in your system, all those microcreatures, have garnered much attention lately. There used to be a time, not so long ago, when we thought killing all the little creatures, internally and externally, as in taking antibiotics or sterilizing everything in your home, was the way to go—the Lysterine and Clorox way. We took hygiene to the extreme, inside and out.

Now we are learning that we are living in dependent coexistence with our microbiome, which is the entirety of all the little microorganisms in our body. We are beginning to understand that a well-populated and diverse gut and intestinal microbiome is the basis for a healthy immune system. Hence fermented foods have become all the rage—yogurt, kombucha, sauerkraut, kimchi, miso, pickled vegetables, sourdough bread—because they all add to, and diversify, our gut bacteria.

In that regard researchers have noticed that Amish children, who grow up in a farming environment, are less susceptible to the more and more prevalent asthma and allergies that children experience who spend much of their time indoors.

So, cultivate your microbiome, don't sweat the small stuff, such as a piece of bread that fell on the floor, or a lettuce leaf that still has a bit of dirt on it; it all helps to "grow more hair on your chest," or strengthen your immune system.

No size fits all   July 18, 2017

You are unique; your digestive system is unique; your food preferences are unique; your constitution, in combination with ethnic provenance and health history, is unique.

It's okay to critically read books on diet trends (paleo, ketogenic, vegan, vegetarian, flexitarian, ethnic), or on nutrition, in order to become informed on the state of our food and its profound influence on our well-being. But then you need to test these theories mindfully on your own body to understand what agrees with you and what doesn't, what aggravates certain conditions or alleviates them, what gives you energy, what regulates your weight, what helps you heal. The one exception I'll take is refined sugar. It's not good for anybody. Period.

We like to simplify and standardize, but imagine what would happen if some diet fundamentalist prescribed the same diet for all seven billion people on this planet? Digestive systems have adapted over hundreds and thousands of years to what is available geographically. Prescribe a vegetarian diet to an Inuit, or an Inuit diet to a Hindu—okay, these are extreme analogies—and they would likely become ill.

So, take all you read, all that people say, with a grain of salt—then see what *really* applies to your own condition and constitution. Although I had already cut out a lot of grain from my diet (and lost quite a bit of weight in the process), I am currently trying this gluten-free thing. I'm really not convinced this is necessary for me—we'll see, hoping to prove myself wrong. No diet applies to all—which one is the right one for you?

Meditations on savoring life
and being in the moment

Not in the moment. . .   April 5, 2012

Just messed up my mayonnaise because I was not in the moment. While I was making macaroni and cheese, I also attempted to make mayonnaise. So much for multitasking. Multitasking is way overrated and does not work (I have actually been preaching that for years now, just need to remember it myself sometimes). In order to finish with the mayonnaise at the same time as the macaroni, I rushed streaming the oil in—and it collapsed and became runny. Waste of eggs and oil, waste of time. I always wonder about multitasking when I watch women in the supermarket on their cellphones. They don't actually shop and phone at the same time, they usually stop in the middle of the aisle, or slow their movements to slow motion, then they resume shopping when they are done with the conversation.

Being in the moment and concentrating on one single thing at a time accomplishes so many things: we do whatever we do deeply, we do it well, and we do it wholeheartedly, something like meditation in motion. I'll remember that when I redo my mayonnaise this afternoon.

Mindful chopping   April 19, 2012

I love cooking and all the prep work that goes with it. Sometimes I even like the prep work more than the rest of the cooking process. It is meditative to me, the peeling, cutting, dicing, and slicing. At the end of the day I spend quiet time with myself in the kitchen, pour myself a glass of wine, and begin preparing dinner. Because my life is *so* busy these days, my dinner-making process is usually somewhat unplanned and spontaneous. I plant myself in front of the fridge, contemplate all the vegetables, fruits, meat or fish (if I thawed something), and staples, and figure out what kind of a meal I can conjure up. Then comes the mindful part, the part where I could almost forget that I am supposed to make a meal for my family, when chopping becomes an activity in its own right. Peeling, chopping, dicing, sipping, whoosh into the pot, and all over again, peeling, chopping, dicing. . .very relaxing and grounding at the end of a busy day.

Sthira and sukha   April 26, 2012

A few days ago, one of my yoga teachers spoke about the yogic concepts of *sthira* and *sukha*. The Sanskrit word *sthira* means grounded or relaxed alertness, while *sukha* is a certain ease. When I think of a professional violinist, a Japanese calligrapher, a martial artist, or anyone else accomplished in their discipline, I see those qualities in them. That combination of in-the-momentness and effortlessness arises out of years of dedicated practice and results in profound perfection.

When I see a classical ballerina dancing on stage, it looks easy, but oh, boy, is it impossible to do what she does without years and years of hard work. We can extend the goal of striving for *sthira* and *sukha* in yoga to striving for it in life. Moreover, the gradual development and achievement of these two qualities in any one area or discipline will inevitably spread into and begin to permeate all other areas of our life.

Take your time zooming   July 2, 2012

. . .my husband said yesterday when I exclaimed I was going to zoom to the farmer's market to pick up a few things and be right back to make breakfast. Although he almost never sits still, he is the one who keeps reminding me to slow down and smell the roses.

The subject of living in the moment keeps creeping up for me. Watching the fabulous fireworks in our town on Saturday night, the thought popped up that fireworks must be the one thing, outside of meditation, where I cannot be other than entirely in the moment. The minute I think about what I see there is already something else to see. So I have to suspend my thinking to keep up with the enjoying.

Just being
October 19, 2012

Usually I am just doing. Dipping under the radar of doingness accesses a place within me that is peaceful, timeless, and emotionally removed (not remote!). This place permits me to observe more objectively without all the emotional entanglement, and it lets me feel, hear, taste, smell, and see without the mental word chatter that permeates my mind. It is difficult to even achieve seconds of this peace of mind, but boy, is it worthwhile.

Working smart, not hard
February 12, 2013

This country was built on the hard-working pioneer spirit that persevered over adverse conditions with dogged determination. Stretching the workday to all hours, eating lunch at the desk, refraining martyr-like from taking vacations, are all still remnants of this dedication in my mind. But times have changed. Working smart, not hard, is the new paradigm. Recent research suggests that we are much more productive working in a few ninety-minute intervals with breaks in between, taking our vacations, and getting enough sleep and recreational time.

This mirrors what spiritual disciplines mean when they say that we need to "slow down in order to speed up."

Why is "now" so important?
March 6, 2013

Because if we are not "here," then we live either in the future or in the past, and what good is that for? "Now" is when things are happening, when we experience joy, pain, fear, and whatnot, "Now" is when life happens. The constant babbling brook of thought running in the background, which we fall prey to, are used to, and take for granted, prevents us from being in the "now."

But it doesn't have to be so; the mind is trainable. I read about a South American shaman who had the opposite problem. He could not understand our Western frazzledness and was trying to comprehend how our minds function, because he only lives in the "now."

Actually, the ideal would be to be able to go back and forth between both mindsets. We need the Western capability of analyzing the past and mapping out where we want to go in the future—to make a plan with intent—and we need the native "Being-in-the-now" for all other times, when we are doing and being. For inspiration take a look at Eckhart Tolle's *Power of Now*, as well as the *Pachamama Alliance* and the *Eagle and Condor Story*.

Making cat cupcakes   July 30, 2013

I am the first culprit when it comes to what I am going to say now, although I have worked my whole life towards what Confucius supposedly said: "Choose a job you love, and you will never have to work a day in your life." In general we need to play more in order to enjoy more. We, as a culture, are rusty at playing—at least I am. Much of life seems to be a chore. So when my daughter made cat cupcakes a few days ago—because she loves cats, and she loves to bake—it reminded me of how little I play. I am just not silly enough (my excuse is that seriousness is in my astrological profile, something about Saturn I think—but then the scientists have already proven that DNA is not static, and that we can change our nature and our biology).

Martha Beck says, in her *Finding Your Way In A Wild New World*, "the way to cope with the increasing complexity of the wild new world is to play more." When we are happily doing and forget about the thinking—whether we dance, sing, make art, make music, play with our children, write a poem, make cat cupcakes—that's play.

Now all we need to do is figure out how to make doing the laundry, or driving the kids all over town, or commuting, or any number of chore-like activities a playful thing. Any thoughts?

Forget your watch   August 30, 2013

I did not take a watch on our recent camping trip. It really did not matter what time I woke up and climbed out of the tent, what time I sipped tea and ate breakfast, what time I went biking or ate lunch. You can actually tell pretty accurately by the sun's standing in the sky, and the quality of the sunlight, about what time it is — not that it really matters when you're on vacation. It is nice to just let yourself float through the day by your feelings of hunger or need for rest or activity.

The accounting of time, and its equation with money, robs time of its magical qualities—and us of our connection with Nature. Charles Eisenstein writes that John Zerzan thought, "Clocks make time scarce and life short." Remember when childhood summer afternoons stretched languorously and lazily into eternity? I am sure it has happened to you that you had to get something specific done in a fairly short amount of time—and managed somehow magically to accomplish it within that tight timeframe. Swedish children's book author Astrid Lindgren wrote in *The Children of Noisy Village* that the endless Christmas Eve afternoons are responsible for our gray hair because they stretch on forever and ever and ever. Similarly, you might have seen Salvador Dali's famous painting of the stretchy clocks.

It's Labor Day weekend. Put your watch away and enjoy time without accounting for it.

An attitude of gratitude   September 9, 2013

How about thinking of life as a gift, as author Charles Eisenstein suggests? What an extraordinary opportunity, what a biological coincidence, what a marvel that you find yourself incarnated in this body, in this place, during these times which Harvard psychologist Steven Pinker has called the most peaceful on Earth yet (despite what the media coverage might suggest).

Think about this opportunity as a gift to experience life on this beautiful Earth, a gift to express your spiritual self in this three-dimensional realm through all the things you do, a gift to share your life with all the people you choose to have around you. This perspective creates an attitude of a half-full glass instead of a half-empty glass, an attitude of gratitude, an attitude of joy, amazement, and wonder. Research suggests that people with a positive outlook on life, a good social network, and a can-do attitude have a longer life expectancy. So from that perspective alone it's worth being grateful.

What if life were really only about the actual experience and joy of being?

Homemade   October 29, 2013

I was so happy when our daughter came back from an event on Saturday and announced that she had won first prize for her Halloween costume. She had sewn the costume herself (with the help of her sewing teacher), which was part of the reason she won.

We have always made our own Halloween costumes. "We" has meant "me" when the children were smaller, although I also remember my husband getting involved. When our son was five, I made him a robot costume out of aluminum-foil-clad boxes, including boxy shoes, while my husband wired the costume up so it would blink. The costume was so impractical that our son had to leave his shoes at the side pf the road because he couldn't walk in them, and he couldn't see too well through the boxy box head's cut-out eyes (good try—but we really had fun making it).

Holistic living is about living in the moment and enjoying it, it's about authentic, or deep living. Sewing your own costume instead of buying one is so much more satisfying. Our daughter got a great sense of accomplishment and empowerment from it, she had a good time while she was making the costume, and she learned a valuable skill along the way. Meanwhile, I got the satisfaction that I taught the children a valuable lesson. What would we have gotten out of a purchased costume? A shopping trip (blah), and money and time not well spent (okay, so the sewing lesson cost as much as a purchased costume), and probably (almost) the same amount of time spent (okay, a bit more—it took her four hours to sew the cat outfit).

Whether it's making jam, cooking dinner, sewing something, tending to a vegetable garden, or building your own bookshelf, it's time better spent (in my opinion) than screen time or shopping-and-driving-around time because it develops a hands-on skill, the activity itself is enjoyable, and the result is handmade and unique.

Oh, beautiful perfect normal day   November 2, 2013

Let's honor and enjoy this great day. Its normalcy is what makes it cherishable—nothing out of the ordinary, no upset, no catastrophe, just quiet and uneventful day-to-day normalcy. Of course, there would be no such day if it weren't for other types of days in contrast, since we live in a yin-yang world, a world where night comes inevitably after day, and is followed again by night, in a never-ending succession. So inevitably, uneventful days will alternate with eventful or upsetting days, exciting days, or crazy busy days.

Today is peaceful and restful, and perhaps even a bit boring and just right.

Beautiful gift wrap November 22, 2013

A relative of mine wasn't much into gift wrapping. As a matter of fact, sometimes she'd come with a bag full of Christmas presents and ask me to wrap them for her because she knew I enjoy doing it.

Why bother with wrapping a present? The short answer is to make magic. The long answer goes something like this. Although we suppress our childlike enthusiasm later in life too often we love surprises (that's for the recipient), and we like to play (that's for the giver who gets to wrap), and we also enjoy watching the look of joy and surprise on the recipient's face. Besides, most of us enjoy beautiful things.

I think a beautifully wrapped present increases manifold in its perceived value. A little trinket can become downright precious with the right wrapping. I guess I shouldn't say this too loudly—but I oftentimes buy relatively inexpensive presents (quality of course, no junk! perhaps something on sale, perhaps something small, perhaps a homemade food item), and make it look really special and precious with creative gift wrapping. It's the thought and the intent behind the gift that counts more than the item's price tag.

The Japanese—who have a very well developed sense of aesthetics—have perfected the art of gift wrapping. One way is to wrap presents in cloth, the art of *furoshiki*. They also have a special way with paper, called *tsutsumi*.

When Christmas comes around and I need to wrap lots and lots of presents I make a special event out of it for myself; some Christmas music, all of the paper, ribbons, gift tags and accessories spread on the floor and table, a cup of tea or a glass of wine—and then I create and wrap. I get to play and make it all look beautiful, and the recipient gets eye candy. It's another quality of life idea. Enjoyment all around.

Glorious color   February 25, 2014

I love color. Color in food, color in clothing, color on my walls, color in Nature. Color makes life sparkle. Many years ago I tried that architect-designer look of wearing lots of black. But that's stark. When my son was little the clothing choices for boys in the mainstream stores were pretty much limited to grey, blue, and brown—how drab.

Of course, color exists only in contrast to black and white, so we need the drabness, the starkness, the dullness, to appreciate color all the more. I think that's why people in cold climates expand in their beingness and start to breathe again when spring comes around, when all that brown-gray-white drabness explodes into greens and pinks and yellows. It is so joyful.

The other day we got blue potatoes from our food co-op. Besides all the added antioxidants, compared to those in white potatoes (although I simply bought them for variety), they looked so pretty on the table. Children often like the safe beige-brown diet (bread, noodles, potatoes, meat).

I say I want color on my table. I also want color in my wardrobe. While red is my favorite color of all, I also love all greens (from Kermit green to a light limy green), all jewel tones (purple, burgundy, burnt yellow, orange, olive green), and creamy yellows.

Live a little, make a splash, and bring some color in your life. It makes life more cheerful.

More focus, less effort   April 1, 2014

In yoga we learn to listen in on our body and feel it, to hold a posture for several breaths, and breathe into the muscles that are being worked. While yoga builds strength over time, it is not about straining to push myself to the limit, but rather about finding that perfect balance between ease and effort. The best thing I recently became aware of was my yoga teacher's suggestion to notice those particular muscles that do the work during a specific asana or posture, and then to relax all the other muscles that are *not* involved (especially the facial muscles, which are usually not involved, yet tense up with all the other muscles). This takes a conscious effort because we tend to tense *all* the muscles indiscriminately. But it is quite a revelation to be able to let go of the strain in most of your body and then precisely concentrate on where the effort actually needs to happen. Instead of being all over the place it takes a lot less effort.

More focus, less effort—and not only in yoga.

Treat yourself   April 4, 2014

It's not always about money or what money can buy. Sure, that luxury spa day makes you feel pampered. But it also costs a ton of money, and that's not what this is about. It's about spending quality quiet time with yourself. And you can do that in many forms, and most of them cost nothing.

How about a bubble bath before going to bed or out to dinner? Or ten minutes of meditation (you can find guided meditations online if you don't trust yourself to stay focused—check out the Chopra Center's free guided meditations). Spending time watering my indoor plants is kind of a meditative quiet time for me; I love to discover new air roots and flower spikes emerging from my orchids.

As a matter-of-fact, I enjoy writing this blog post right now. So in a way I am treating myself. So what is something you will be doing for yourself? Have a glass of wine—and be sure to drink it out of a beautiful glass.

The soft glow of candles   May 9, 2014

I love candles. The more the merrier. Lit, of course. There is something mystical about a live flame—the flickering, the color range from blue to white to yellow, then orange, and the changing length of the flame depending on the wick and how it burns. Candle watching can be quite mesmerizing and meditative. But what I think I like most about candlelight is the soft and uneven glow it lends to the surrounding space. It adds more depth than the even and flat light of a lamp.

"Mom, can I blow the candles out?" Before children are allowed to light them they want to blow them out. *Poof.* Then they graduate to being allowed to light them with adult supervision. Perhaps you remember how special it was when you allowed your child to light a candle for the first time?

Candles are another one of those quality-of-life things that we should use more often. Outdoor candlelight in the summer feels different from indoor candlelight in the winter. Candlelight adds magic to so many different settings. I like to light a candle when I take a bath. It makes me feel pampered. Sometimes I light a candle on my desk when I work, it gives it a special feel, it seems to soften the energy. When I light candles on the table for a birthday breakfast, a celebratory dinner, or a dinner party, it not only makes it look festive, it also sends the message, *It's special.*

Christmastime is a time for red candles—on the tree (yes, we use real candles in special German holders that screw directly into the tree trunk), on our Advent wreath, and throughout the house. A special table setting will look great with colored tapers to match the decor. Most other times I like the elegant glow of off-white candles.

Flickering candles on the picnic table on a hot summer night make the world stop in its tracks. I like the soft glow of candles in weighted paper bags along a walkway, on some rocks in the garden, or on a beach. Two summers ago in Italy, when their grandma was not well, the children lit a candle for her in every church we visited. At Halloween tea lights in little and big hollowed-out and carved pumpkins, inside the house and outside, announce the beginning of the dark season that candles help to brighten so beautifully. I like lots of tea lights placed in clusters or rows. It's like tulips— one looks skimpy, lots make a statement. And no birthday table in our house is complete without that special single lit birthday candle and a bouquet of seasonal flowers.

Enjoy your weekend, really   May 23, 2014

What is it always with this Thursday or Friday frenzy before a long weekend? The pace picks up frenetically, everyone seems to need something very urgently before close of business, nothing can wait until after the weekend—as if we were closing shop for the next three weeks. But in light of the fact that we are back on Tuesday morning it's really quite absurd. Many things can wait, and how is a three-day weekend so different from the regular two-day weekend anyhow?

In this country—and in Hong Kong, where I lived for a bit as well—many people feel guilty about taking time off. Culturally, virtue is seen in working long hours (even if they are not all so productive), slaving away (or looking as if you are) for the bottom line, bowing to the Grand Poobah of profitability and money, and fearing job loss otherwise. Many European countries give between four and six weeks' vacation (on top of the many religious holidays and sick leave), and their economies are doing just fine.

We need time off to clear our head, to sleep in, to get out of the *métro-boulot-dodo* routine (French for the never-ending subway-work-sleep grind), pursue our hobbies, and spend time with family and friends. Time off refreshes us, it balances us, it puts things into perspective. Lack of sleep and too much stress shorten our lifespan. Without playtime life is dull and drudgery.

Time off is a necessity in order to perform optimally and creatively; it's not frivolous luxury. Enjoy your weekend, and don't feel guilty about your time off.

It's not about the destination   June 3, 2014

There are various English versions of the destination verse, which goes something like this, "It's not about the destination, it's about the journey." When I was in elementary school many girls kept a *Poesiealbum* or "poetry album." We would give it to people we knew—family, classmates, teachers, acquaintances—and ask them to write something to remember them by. Some of the verses, as I reread them, mostly from classmates, are memorable only because of their utter silliness, while others (mostly from teachers and family members) are true philosophical musings or really good life advice.

I found one in my album by the 19th-century Austrian writer Marie von Ebner-Eschenbach, which is another version of the destination verse. Loosely translated, it says, "Upon attaining your wishes, you will definitely miss one thing, the journey towards your wish."

If life was only about the destination we would all rush to accomplish—what? Dying? So we can probably all agree that life is not about the destination. But what about all the other little things we do all day long? This morning my yoga class was a bit strenuous, and I just wanted it to be over—until I caught myself in mid-stream. And then I recognized that I wasn't doing so badly, and that I was actually gaining strength.

It's not worth doing something if we rush right past it. Granted, there are things we enjoy doing, and there are things we don't enjoy doing; and it's good if you can arrange your life so you can do more things you *do* enjoy, than things you *don't* enjoy. But things are easier with less resistance, as I experienced this morning. And when it's over, it's really over.

So, stay with the moment, with the experience, because none like it exactly will ever come back.

Let's celebrate   July 3, 2014

Sometimes it's not so much about *what* we celebrate than *that* we celebrate. We make up reasons to celebrate to lift ourselves out of the rut, day-to-day life, the ordinary. Think yin and yang. Whether it's a birthday, a milestone, or a national holiday—they are all great reasons to celebrate.

We thrive on being with people, sharing food with people, talking with people, doing things with people. And that's what celebrations are about. Getting out of the office, out of bed, out of everyday life, and making an effort. Of course, it's more of an effort if the celebration is at your own house than if you are just visiting somewhere. But we all take turns between being invited and being hosts. And why not look at party prep time as playtime, using the reason for the celebration as a theme for food and decorations, and even games. I know people who knock themselves out with party themes so it all matches, food included. That can be a lot of fun.

On quietude   July 11, 2014

We have been living in a very old house in the countryside, on a fairly busy road, for the past two decades. Before that, we lived in New York City, where you hear car alarms and fire trucks at all hours, and where there is always background noise. As a matter of fact, except for a few years when I was young, I have always lived in big noisy cities. You do get used to the constant background noise, but it becomes like a chronic illness. After a while you only notice how noisy it is when there is silence in between.

I know they say that quiet comes from within. But then they also say that we create what we connect with, what we need, and what we are attracted to. When I was young I was always looking for inspiration from the outside—travel, experiences, moving to yet another place, or starting another career. You can create a certain amount of inner quiet, but at one point or another peace and quiet are helpful for tuning out chatter, staying grounded, concentrating on your work, and promoting peace and balance.

It is wonderfully grounding and balancing to just sit in Nature with no other noises than chirping birds, buzzing bees, the wind quietly sweeping through the grass, or the waves of a lake lapping at the shore—and between such breaks in the utter silence, nothing. No electronic beeps and alerts, no planes overhead (just heard one), no cars passing by (several just drove past), no phones ringing (yep, just rang), no kitchen machines running in the background (I hear the faint noise of the dishwasher humming). All those mechanical human-made sounds are less harmonious to our ears and grate at you after a while.

Inner and outer silence makes room for creativity, for concentration, for going deep within. It's what they mean by a *pregnant pause*—the in-between space, the space that came before the Big Bang. This space is empty but so full of potential. I am looking forward to this quietude as a basis for increased creativity in the coming years. When I open the windows in our new house all I hear is birds singing, the wind swishing through the trees, and occasionally the neighbor's rooster crowing (ah, such a European countryside sound to my ears—love it). Pure bliss.

Music to my ears   *July 22, 2014*

Sounds, just like comforting smells, say of freshly baked apple pie for example, can trigger and evoke memories. It's as if the sound lodged itself in our cells and replayed certain memories, emotions, or situations from the past that get triggered on command. That way we come to associate a particular sound or piece of music with a particular memory, pleasant or not.

The neighbors across from us have a rooster that crows on occasion. I love that sound. The crowing evokes for me the European countryside, together with peacefulness and that dreamy quality of a summer morning or of a languorous Sunday lunch that comes to an end. When I told our neighbor I loved the sound of her rooster she was so happy, saying apologetically that she had thought it might bother people. Not me.

Church bells also bring back nostalgic European childhood memories for me. Over here we don't hear church bells much, and if we do many are electronic, which removes the charm of the sound. But in Europe church bells still sound regularly on the hour, or at least on Sundays, not only in small villages but also in big cities. It is a comforting sound to me.

What sounds trigger pleasant memories for you?

Let go of the breaks   October 10, 2014

We cling to predictability, trying to find safety in laws and ordinances (there are more of them every day; what a morass to navigate and enforce), and more warning labels come out all the time. From notifications about how to wear your bike helmet safely, to signs meant to prevent young children from ingesting small toy parts, from signs to keep us from jumping into a three foot deep pool, to labeling your nut free cereal that it was processed in a facility that does process tree nuts, to shots that are supposed to safeguard us from everything and anything (and there are more of those all the time as well), and insurance for everything, including life (although that one can't give you your life back if you lose it). We have become a society obsessed with safety.

Most of us want to be in total control of our life, prevent it from bringing us unpredictable situations, rolling along nicely and rather boringly (and then people go on these crazy adventure vacations where they can live a bit that letting go in a somewhat controlled environment and under supervision—so ironic).

They say, "What doesn't kill you makes you stronger." It is only natural that we wouldn't willingly and knowingly subject ourselves to some of the harder lessons we may have learned, although in hindsight these may turn out to have been valuable contributions to build character or, as my husband would say, "build hair on our chest."

On the flip side, this cautiousness and timidity prevent us from living life to the fullest and may keep some beautiful opportunities at bay the universe may otherwise send our way in its infinite wisdom. There are many situations where I couldn't have planned things better than the universe did for me. Our move this past summer ended up happening almost simultaneously with the closing on our old house. Yet we put the house on the market back in the fall of last year for fear of not finding a buyer in time. If we really had sold the house any earlier, either we or the buyer would have been in trouble.

I often now put out to the universe a wish for the most benevolent outcome of a particular situation. And then I watch and see what happens and let things unfold. Trust yourself, trust the universe, try sending out this "most benevolent thing," but refrain from putting the breaks on life too much. You might just miss out on some beautiful moments and some great opportunities.

Making magic   December 23, 2014

Here a thought that was inspired—yet again—by my beautiful yoga teacher, who always has so many words of wisdom. She was referring to Corinthians 4:18: "So we fix our eyes not on what is seen, but on what is unseen, since what is seen is temporary, but what is unseen is eternal."

She suggested to keep in mind during this Christmas season that it is the unseen, the invisible, that makes magic. What is in our hearts makes magic, the love we share is magic, the time we spend with friends and family is magic, sparkles in the children's eyes when they open their presents is magic, the joy of being part of a greater whole is magic, our family traditions and rituals during this time are magic, our ethnic connections and family ties make magic, the thought behind a truly thoughtful present makes magic, neighborly appreciation makes magic, kindness and compassion make magic.

May you experience lots of magic, and may you make lots of magic during this holiday season.

A seasonal winter display   February 3, 2015

What a visually pleasing tradition to have a seasonal display at home, not only when there is a particular holiday but simply to remind us of the current season. The display might include some plant or Nature element, such as a bare branch in the wintertime, maybe some pretty rocks, perhaps a candle—really anything that reflects the current time of year, the mood, and what it means to you.

A fireplace mantel lends itself beautifully to this kind of display because it is usually so centrally placed in the home. But a side table in the entrance, a pedestal in the dining room, or a window alcove in the living room are all just as suitable. When my children were small, they went to a Waldorf nursery school, where it is customary to have such a display on a table in the playroom.

The Japanese traditionally have a *tokonoma* in their home, a niche with a seasonal scroll, a seasonal flower display, perhaps a candle and some incense, all thoughtfully selected.

Consider taking a look around your garden and your house,

and think about a few items to place in a location you pass a few times a day. It might become a spot where you stop just for a second to pause and interrupt the flow of things.

Comforting rituals   April 3, 2015

Ritual is something that's "always done in a particular situation and in the same way each time," according to Merriam-Webster's online dictionary. Rituals that come to mind are daily ones (getting up, taking a shower, going to bed), religious ones (mass, prayer), and rituals connected to specific occasions (holiday celebrations, funerals, last day of school).

My (almost) daily ritual is to shut the computer after a day's work, go down to the kitchen, and begin cooking dinner while sipping a glass of wine. Brushing my teeth as soon as I get out of bed is a ritual too, because I do it every day, in the same way, with the same movements. But the rituals I really want to talk about, on the cusp of this Passover/Easter weekend, are the special ones for special occasions.

Why do we create and need ritual? Ritual is reassuring, and we need certain routines in life. It is reassuring to know how, when, and in what fashion, to celebrate an occasion, instead of inventing it anew each time. Annual holiday rituals tie us to Nature's cycles as well as to our ethnic culture and roots. Like the seasons that always come back every year in the same sequence, like the moon that waxes and wanes always in the same predictable way, rituals are grounding specifically because they don't change. There is reassurance in knowing what to expect because the rest of life is so full of change, adjustment, fluctuation, and surprises.

It is especially comforting for children to learn and have rituals because they create rhythm and help them to find their place in the world—in Nature, in their culture, in their family. My Easter menu doesn't change much from year to year. It's always a leg of lamb, always asparagus and some other green springtime vegetables. I ritualistically buy a white hyacinth every year a few weeks before Easter, and we all associate its smell, which permeates the entire house, with Easter and the beginning of spring. Each year, about three weeks before Easter, we bring up the Easter storage box from the basement to pull out the painted eggs and decorate pussy willow or other bare branches, which will start to sprout tender leaves by Easter.

Same thing each year. Here's to a new spring.

Make it special   April 14, 2015

Splurging is only splurging, and treating myself is only a treat, if I don't do it all the time. Otherwise it's excess, or habit, or addiction. When you treat yourself for every little excuse, whether it's with shopping, or eating sweets, or something else, it's no longer special. And then it's no longer fun. You only feel special when it's *really* special. I believe that it's important to splurge and treat yourself every once in a while, constantly being a miser is miserable.

My daughter's special reward for a good math test used to be a sweet afternoon treat with a cup of rich hot chocolate at our wonderful French pâtisserie. But then she got to be very good at math, and we went to the pâtisserie very often, and then it wasn't special anymore. So we had to redefine those rewards. Meat used to be special; hence the traditional Sunday roast. If you have meat every day, and lots, it quickly becomes an unhealthy addiction. Going out for dinner is special. Yet if you do it all the time it loses its luster. We went to a Broadway show this past weekend. That was very special. As a matter of fact, it was my daughter's first Broadway show (that's how rarely we do it). And it felt like a real splurge.

Make it special and make it rare. It will sparkle a lot more.

Deeply experiencing   April 22, 2015

After a long winter indoors, it feels so good to be outside, open your arms wide in exuberance, and breathe in the fresh moist spring air in big gulps. *Ahh*. . .smelling the air is a thrilling experience, just like digging into the dirt and feeling the soil crumble in your hands, touching the tender spring flowers and shoots that are coming up out of the ground, seeing the fresh spring colors emerging, and listening to the gentle breeze whooshing in the trees.

What we don't usually realize is that all of these sensations occur simultaneously. What a much deeper experience to pause and take all of these impressions in together, the way they actually occur. When you are fully in that moment with Nature, it becomes an overwhelmingly complex, almost dizzying meditation. How does that moment feel then?

On the other hand, when we dissect a moment's experience into the different names we give it—hearing the breeze, smelling the fresh air, feeling the tender shoots, seeing the fresh colors— we experience these sensations consecutively. The separation occurs because we put the sensations into words, which inherently happen consecutively, and because we think about them. We can't simultaneously think about three different sensations that happen at the same time. Impossible. But we can experience them if we become still, get the words out of the way, and just be.

Just being makes you shift from seeing the world in consecutive flat segments to a complex holographic whole.

Awesome details   June 29, 2015

The advice not to lose the forest for the trees is generally a good one because the big picture frames our perspective and reminds us not to get lost in minutiae. This is especially practical advice when trying to get something accomplished. Yet you may miss out on some hidden jewels.

Contemplating Nature's details can be a deeply meditative activity. I am always amazed at the intricate and delicate details of my orchid blossoms. Nature creates such incredible complexity on such a micro level, it's awe inspiring. It's also easy to pass by without noticing it. Looking at a spray of phalaenopsis orchid blossoms from afar, you will miss the details. But get down on your knees—so to speak—and the colors of the orchid center alone are spectacular—orange, crimson red, lime green, and lemon yellow, set against a porcelain-white background. And how about the shapes, tiny as they are? So elaborate, so intricate. Look at the two wispy filigreed extensions that start out white and end in a curled yellow spiral. Or the yellow-and-red striped part in the throat of the orchid. Or the orange pad (is it the stigmatic surface?) with the red dots in the very center. And did you notice the see-through holes the petal shapes are creating? Or the interesting shape of the lip, the protruding part the insect would land on?

Ultimately the names of the parts don't matter at all. It is about the experience of savoring the exquisite details and colors inside the otherwise so sculpturally white orchid that gives me such pleasure when I walk past the flower that I need to stop and tell it how beautiful, how perfect it is.

Of course you can contemplate other shapes in nature and be awed—moss for example, or crystals, or a butterfly's wings. There is endless beauty, perfection, and intricacy to be found all around. Each one merits its own attention.

More time for lunch   July 21, 2015

"Madame," the waiter in the small town of Amboise in France said to me with a serious face, "I cannot serve you if you don't have enough time for lunch." My daughter and I were on a breathtaking whirlwind group tour through France and Spain and had a two-thirty château visit scheduled. We had just breezed into town from Chartres. It was a quarter to two when we sat down in the little sidewalk café, and I had just told the waiter that we had forty-five minutes for lunch—not a lot.

Well, the French like to take their time with meals, and rightfully so—have their wine, linger, and chat, especially on the weekend. And here I'd come to tell the waiter to rush, on a Saturday of all days. It went very much against his grain as well as mine. I hate to rush meals. As a matter of fact, I hate to rush, period. Life doesn't get much better than a lazy summer lunch in a small French town in a small restaurant, choosing whatever house special is on the blackboard that day—a delicious tuna tartare one day, this time a big salad with roasted pork belly and local goat cheese, another time grilled squid and vegetables and an octopus salad, a glass of wine from the area, watching the people passing by, listening to the birds, and enjoying the fantastic weather.

Life is better when it's slow.

Tiring or inspiring?   November 20, 2015

Kris Carr, the crazy sexy cancer guru, whom I heard at last weekend's Hay House I-Can-Do-It Conference, proposed a very easy way to tap into your intuition about a situation or an activity or your job you are not sure about. She suggested asking yourself whether it tires or inspires you.

Emotions and feelings are easy and sure indicators of where you stand with things, although they are not well understood. It seems we don't quite know what to do with them. Wouldn't life be easier if we didn't have any emotions? Guys used to be raised that way—be tough, don't show your pain, just forget her, there'll be others. So we tend to ignore our feelings, bury them, or criticize ourselves for having them. But cell biologist Bruce Lipton assured us during that same conference that "feelings are a more accurate description of life than thoughts."

That means that we can use them as indicators; they provide us with valuable information. Do you love being at your job and doing whatever it is that you do? Are you challenged, appreciated, and energized? Or do you feel tired and drained at the end of the day, wishing for a different way to earn your daily bread? Does your partner in crime inspire you, lift your spirits, and show his appreciation for who you are? Or not so much? Do you love to go to the gym and derive great energy from it? Or do you dread going to the gym because you do it out of a sense of obligation? Nancy Levin wrote in one of her poems, "it's a sign of healing to be feeling." Feelings are very practical road signs to help you navigate life.

The human touch   March 22, 2016

Most of the time I feel a bit guilty when I take care of myself (and call it pampering). But massages actually accomplish several worthwhile things besides being a pure indulgence. For one you get total downtime (your only obligation is to show up, lie on the table, enjoy, and think sweet thoughts), you also reconnect with your body, get to enjoy the pleasures of caring human touch, and last but not least, knots and tension dissolve under the massage therapist's knowledgeable hands. Author and physician Christiane Northrup writes, "Touch is a basic human need, so meet it shamelessly." Did you know that gentle touch actually releases the pleasure hormone oxytocin and melts away stress?

It's easy to make excuses, especially the money kind. Consider swapping a massage for something you do well through an hour-exchange. No money spent. What better way to spend thirty or sixty minutes?

On contentment   April 6, 2016

I feel content right now. Contentment is a feeling that leaves nothing wanting. The current moment is perfect. I am deeply relaxed and everything is alright. It feels peaceful, and somewhat meditative, as nothing is rushing in on me that needs immediate attention or couldn't wait. It is somewhat of a mild feeling, nothing like exuberance, joy, or exhilaration, more like a quiet happiness that is deeply satisfying. I feel it after a yoga session, I feel it when I am not under pressure, and I feel it right now. I hope it'll last a bit.

When was the last time you felt contentedness?

Doing instead of watching   August 30, 2016

Cooking shows are really popular these days, as are all kinds of reality shows, and of course sports events. But watching something is a step removed from living. It's an activity that engages the mind, not the entire body—heart and soul included. Watching doesn't engage the whole you. It's disengaged, detached. It's like grazing versus digging. That's why they say that we learn by doing.

When I sit in front of the screen and watch a cooking show, I may ooh and aah, I may be inspired, but I am not deeply engaged because I don't *do*. When I stand in the kitchen chopping, sautéing, saucing, tasting, spicing, smelling, creating, I'm in the zone because I'm *doing*. When I watch a dance routine I may be amazed, but I'm an observer of someone one else having all the fun. When I dance myself I'm inside myself, I am the action, I am the dancing, I am having the fun—I am living, I am alive.

Enjoying life and creating meaning is about more doing and less watching.

Radical tidying   September 2, 2016

Marie Kondo's only criterion for keeping anything is whether "the item sparks joy." Her method for uncluttering your home (and your life) has become internationally known through her book *The Life-Changing Magic of Tidying Up*. Kondo's approach to tidying your home promises a whole new mindset once you have gone through her radical process of ridding yourself of everything that doesn't make you feel good. And organizing, she makes clear, cannot start until you have gotten rid of all that excess stuff. She also promises no relapses because your mind will have shifted during this radical process.

Take your wardrobe, for example. You probably have a bunch of items in the back of your closet you haven't worn in years but keep around because you might just sometime feel like wearing them again. Or maybe you feel guilty about getting rid of them because you think that's wasteful (well, think consignment store). But if you do take the time to take each piece into your hands and reflect on whether this piece of clothing makes you feel good when you wear it (Kondo's method), and the answer is a resounding, "Nah, not really," you know what to do. Get rid of it. Same advice goes for your books, nick-knacks, pantry items, and everything else in your house.

I think it's worth a try. Although my home is not cluttered, I know I keep things around that wouldn't pass muster if I asked myself that test question. Kondo's idea, behind all of this radical purging, is to surround yourself only with things you love, and to clear stuck and stale energy in the process, inside and out.

Seeking meaning   October 25, 2016

British author Karen Armstrong said about mankind, "We are meaning-seeking creatures." My cats live day to day without that ongoing quest for a deeper meaning. Sure, sometimes they are happier than other times. But all in all their life is just peachy, without worry or concern, but also without deeper meaning.

As to us, we thrive on meaning. We want to know, "Why?" We invent creation stories to imbue our culture with root beliefs, we create special festivities and attach symbols and customs to them to create significance, we create culture as backdrop for life and as a basis for shared experience, which creates meaning in and of itself.

Consider the two sides of our ongoing search for meaning. We become depressed when we see no meaning, and we thrive when we can glean a deeper significance to what we do. Finding meaning gives us a sense of purpose, and it can propel us and inspire us; lack of meaning can torture us.

In yoga they say, "There is no place to go, you are already here," meaning there is no need to struggle towards some goal we create for ourselves based on some narrative. My cats are already there— right here; they don't look further. We are different, I guess, until we become enlightened; then we're like my cats, content to be right where they are, which is here. Buddhists say that all suffering comes from having desires, and when there are no desires there is no suffering.

What do you think?

Beauty everywhere   November 1, 2016

The other night I cut up some red cabbage to make a salad for dinner . . . and stopped in my tracks. I simply was struck by the beauty, not only of the vivid purple-white color combination, but especially by the intricate patterns that revealed themselves under my knife as I kept cutting through the cabbage wedges. I just had to stop, pull out the camera, and take a few pictures. The swirly, thin, red lines, embedded in larger swaths of white, looked like art to me, like purple switch backs or a brainy kind of pattern. They alternate with straighter white and purple shapes, and the color combination is just gorgeous.

You can find beauty anywhere and in the most unexpected places. Just stop in your tracks and look around. Did you see something beautiful today?

Did you take a big bite? December 28, 2016

Our current perception of time is cut up into segments that start over after each cycle; let's take stock and reboot to begin fresh: 2016 is winding down with the passing of two big stars, Carrie Fisher and George Michael. Neither of them was very old. But a wise soul said to me once not to judge a life by its length but by its meaning.

Here, then, are two messages to take away as this year wanes. Take stock, and look back. What significance did this year have for you? What did you learn? What did you accomplish? What influence have you had on those around you? Did you give? Did you take? Have you gained depth? Compassion? What were the big moments this year for you personally? How do they fit into the bigger scheme of the you-theme? My biggest accomplishment this year was the completion of my book—finally. It will be out this winter.

The message that goes hand in hand with the first one is to live big, to live life to its fullest—my mother-in-law called it "taking a big bite out of life." You can't go back and fix things in the past. But you can shift your mindset right now and make the next moment, and the next day, or month, or year significant. Take a big bite out of life today and this coming year. Make it meaningful, for yourself and others, through your actions.

First coffee, first walk January 3, 2017

On Sunday, first day of the New Year, we had fun marveling at all the firsts we experienced—first cup of tea of the New Year, first breakfast of the New Year, first walk of the New Year, and on and on. It was fun and uplifting. My husband mused about how exciting life would be if we looked at everything we do as "a first," with the sense of wonderment and freshness the New Year brings.

That's the secret of living in the moment! There is always a new day, a new month, a new afternoon, to keep playing this game endlessly. Try it.

Tangoing from the heart   January 13, 2017

A few weeks ago, my husband and I started taking beginner lessons in Argentine tango—the place is only ten minutes from our house, and the lessons happen to be free, major incentives— although we have dabbled in ballroom dancing since before we had kids (always on and off, always at the glorified beginner level).

But tango seems different, less mechanical and structured than conventional ballroom dancing, and more intuitive and sensual. For one there is that sliding, slithering tango walk—the most basic tangoing might actually simply entail slide-walking to tango music. Tango requires dropping from the head into the heart, and isn't that the topic of our times? Tango teaches trust because the follower always moves backward. As a matter of fact, some of the practice exercises were done with closed eyes. More so than conventional ballroom dancing (at least it seems so from my beginner's perspective), tango becomes a complete merging of self, music, and partner, an in-the-moment moving, feeling, trusting, responding to your partner—no anticipation, just being in the now.

Tango, and ballroom dancing in general, are good for your health. They help your balance and coordination, and moving to music is joyful. Tango in particular is also very sensual; it requires and trains trust, it's great exercise that's a lot more fun than running on a treadmill, you can do it 'til the day you die, and as a social activity it connects you with people. As an exercise in togetherness, partnership, and trusting, it's a perfect hobby for our times.

We need to play more, we need to dance more, we need to enjoy life more.

The best art   February 3, 2017

Walls without pictures are naked. Counters, consoles, and bookcases without *tchotchkes* are barren. Visual art pulls a place, whether home or office, together, and gives it that unique touch. Because I am not a visual artist myself, I need other people's art in my life.

Art adds color, art adds interest, art adds meaning, and art adds creativity. Art doesn't have to be expensive, and it sure doesn't have to be from someone famous. As a matter of fact, I like to know the people whose art I hang up or display, and I like to know their stories—I get more meaning from that than I would from an expensive piece whose maker I don't know.

I have saved the best of my children's art from their elementary school years and framed it. A friend's young son made a piece of book art, which I cherish and display together with some super-heavy candlesticks a friend made from farm implements, and a tree study we got from a painter friend. And I love my daughter's African-inspired gazelle head, made in kindergarten from a plastic gallon jug. They are all beautiful pieces that make the room around them look more special, and each piece has a story. This type of art surrounds me with beauty and meaning.

So exquisite   March 21, 2017

Is there anything more beautiful than water drops glittering like Swarovski crystals in the sun? Nature creates this kind of perfection effortlessly, without trying—naturally. So different from us when we try to create beauty. We have to apply skill and technology. We need to work at it, spending years of practicing and perfecting a skill, before something becomes naturally beautiful without trying too hard.

Quality over quantity   May 9, 2017

Racing through the calendar from one appointment to the next, breathlessly looking at the next event as something else to check off the to-do list, makes death your final appointment. "I made it!" But it's too late then to wake up to the realization that your life was one mad dash to the finish line.

Lately, we were caught in a mad routine between accommodating our daughter's many early-evening activities, my occasional evening meetings, our tango lessons, and my husband's attempts to return on time from a busy workday. It became stressful, and our quality of life suffered, especially trying to get dinner in there somewhere, hopefully before the tango lesson, after our daughter's evening activity, before my evening meeting, attempting to eat together, and making a home cooked meal from scratch. . . you get it—exhausting.

Meaning comes from the quality of what we do, whether it's tango, taekwondo, or the made-from-scratch meal. For us the tango had to go, at least for now. It was just too much. We had to choose quality over quantity, depth over breadth.

Scent of a guava   May 17, 2017

Don't judge a book by its cover, they say. This unassuming little fruit, a guava, which I picked up out of curiosity at a Walmart of all places, has a beguiling, strong, and very particular scent.

Scent adds so much depth and pleasure to an experience. The clamshell with eight or so small guavas scented our entire kitchen for a few days, and later on the compost pail from the cut-off top bits. I have seen the scent described as musky, which is perhaps why I found it quite addicting. But I also found it very florally perfumed.

Our sense of taste is informed by our sense of smell; hence, you can't taste when you have a cold. But because we are so visual we often give what we *see* more importance than the messages from our other senses. The sight of these guavas is not exactly special. It is the scent that is so attractive, and it is what made me wonder what they actually taste like. I did remember having eating guava paste, but that is a sorry and sweet treat lacking the lovely brightness of a fresh, perfumed guava.

Realtors talk about the power of the smell of fresh -baked apple pie in closing a house sale, and specific scents can bring back memories in a powerful way. Smells or scents add so much to our aliveness, to the depth of how we know the world.

On nurturing
our planet

Be patient! July 26, 2013

We have become used to instant gratification. Information is now available at the touch of a finger. We no longer write letters, barely even send emails or make telephone calls—we text and tweet. Our attention spans have become shorter, as teachers have noticed, and the movie and TV industries exploit and promote it, which then self-perpetuates.

On the material side the credit system has enabled us to buy now and pay later, since we choose no longer to be patient until we have saved up enough money. Besides houses and cars, we can also get everything else instantly without paying for it up front (just pay Amazon an annual fee, and you'll get two-day shipping on all your orders). We have lost our patience, we live on credit, and we are banking on a better future to acquire today's (perceived) needs now.

The belief that this system will function on a long-term basis is also coloring our relationship with Nature. Many don't want to believe—yet, it seems—that oil and natural gas reserves are finite. Many don't want to believe—yet—that we have a huge garbage problem. Many don't want to believe that we have any number of grave environmental challenges to deal with. We'll fix them in the future—or so many still like to believe. Environmentally speaking, we live thus on credit instead of investing *now* in our environmental future. From indigenous cultures we need to relearn patience and a long-term outlook on issues.

Native Americans look seven generations ahead into the future! We must invest in a viable future for our children, grandchildren, and five more generations out, instead of leaving them to mop up our messes. *The Lorax* is a good book by Dr. Seuss on what happens otherwise.

We are Nature   August 27, 2013

That we have come to think of ourselves as separate from Nature shines through when we say, "Let me take a walk in Nature," or when we refer to Nature as "outside." And of course it shines through in how we treat Nature—we have not been kind to it lately.

As a society we have come to view ourselves as superior to it, as separate from it; we dominate and control Nature, and "use" it for our enrichment. I believe this behavior arose from disassociation and fear—what indigenous person would fear Nature? How absurd; they live with it, in it, as part of it, from it. We Westerners of industrialized nations need to relearn to live with it, understand it, be kind to it, embrace it, and work with it.

What is "Nature," actually? The 1970s gave rise to the idea of the Gaia principle, the idea of Earth as one enormously complex organism that encompasses everything from rocks and rivers, to plants and minerals, to animals and humans. While the Gaia principle excludes elements outside of planet Earth (the planets, the cosmos), it is a step in the right direction of a more encompassing understanding of our embeddedness in Earth. Native American Chief Seattle supposedly said something like, "Whatever you do to the web you do to yourself." We are Nature just as much as trees, mushrooms, mice, whales, clouds, the sun, or our consciousness. And because *we are Nature* we need to relearn to honor it, and we need to learn responsible stewardship of it and ourselves as part of this enormous and intricate web.

Divorce is not an option   October 25, 2013

That's what Bill Clinton said about our interdependence with our planet in his keynote address at Omega Institute's recent conference on sustainability, which I attended. We must all wake up to the fact that climate change is here, that it is real, that it is man-made, that it is happening fast, and that it is a scary thing. As a matter of fact, Jeremy Rifkin, the writer and economic and social visionary, actually called it "terrifying."

But then, out of crisis and chaos new things are born. Environmentalist and entrepreneur Paul Hawken's message, at that same conference, was to embrace carbon, our supposed enemy. "Carbon," he says, "is the business of life and the answer to our nightmares," the subject of a book he is currently writing, because carbon is "the currency of abundance," a concept we lack in our present interest-based economics of scarcity (see also Charles Eisenstein's *Sacred Economics*). Interesting, because spiritual traditions have always advised us to embrace our enemies, who mirror back to us what we lack or need to embrace.

So, since divorce from our planet is not an option, and closing our eyes and ears just prolongs the agony, we each need to wake up—quickly, quickly. The break, or consciousness shift, that the Mayans may have seen in the ending of their calendar with the year 2012 is here. Change is opportunity, and we choose how gently or how chaotically change happens. Through embrace and acceptance, change happens more gently. Do your bit—we must get off carbon as an energy source and embrace it in other forms. Insulate your home, realize that the world is changing, eat much less meat and not the supermarket kind, open up to your intuition, speak kindly to others, and most of all enjoy life! That way, "Life does not come *at* you, it comes *from* you," as my wise yoga teacher said.

It's no longer business as usual!

Watching my plants grow   May 20, 2014

I grew up in big cities, and I still have somewhat of an issue connecting with Nature in a big way—Big Nature, as in wild-water rafting, mountain climbing, several-day bike trips, overnights in a lean-to in the woods, and stuff like that. I don't feel comfortable in *Big Nature* because of a lack of guidance and experience. Instead, I connect with *little Nature* in the form of my houseplants or my vegetable garden.

I get really excited when seedlings emerge from the soil in early spring, and I love accompanying them on their growth journey through the season towards becoming fully grown vegetables. It's a bit like watching your children grow and develop, and change and come into being.

Discovering little green tomatoes among the greenery, and then seeing them grow, grow, grow into big, red, ripe, juicy fruit we can actually eat is awesome and so rewarding. The whole process is a bit magical to me. When I find a ripe zucchini lurking under its big protective leaves, it is like finding a present or a prize. And I love bringing the flowers from the vegetable garden into the house, a bouquet of purple-pink chive flowers, or perhaps a few sprigs of white and gangly arugula flowers together with a few sage flowers.

I don't think it matters how you come to appreciate Nature, how you connect with it, how you come to respect it—as long as you do it in your own way.

The color of life   May 1, 2015

I find the color green very soothing. It seems restful to my eyes. I love when vibrant green begins to mix into the drab gray-browns of winter and gradually take over by the end of May. I can look at an expanse of thick, juicy, green grass forever and feel peaceful. Walking in the woods, I enjoy staring at the dense green tree canopy.

"Green, the result of photosynthesis, which creates all of our food, is the color of life," says Petra Fromme of Arizona State University. The *Times* reported recently that blue and green are the world's favorite colors. Our vision is optimized for green, says Bevil Conway of Wellesley College.

Not only our mind, but our body too, thrives on greens, whether in the form of leafy green vegetables, that miracle healer wheat grass juice (two ounces of it provides as many nutrients as five pounds of raw vegetables—wow!), that other super healer chlorella algae, and various other mineral rich sea vegetables.

On respecting Nature   June 16, 2015

Hearing bear stories and seeing one up close are two different things. A few days ago I observed a bear, out of my office window, playing with a log, meandering along the tree line, trying to get down from the cliff behind our house, then deciding it was too steep, and slowly disappearing back into the woods. Today, I took a—brief—lunchtime walk and saw what I presume was the same bear, slowly crossing the road in the not-so-distant distance. I was in awe and treaded back—hence the brevity of the walk.

Even the Native Americans respect the bear because it is so powerful and can be fickle. It behooves us to respect Nature, to bow in reverence before its grandeur, power, unpredictability, and force, whether Nature comes in animal, plant, weather, or geological form. It seems to me that we, as a culture, have unlearned to work with it, alongside it, leaving it alone when need be, and not walking all over it with disrespect and hubris. When we live away from Nature we tend to see it as something different from us, something we can use and exploit.

But are we not Nature, too?

Greening your thumb   September 9, 2015

I used to have a definite "brown thumb," which has turned to a pretty "green thumb" over the years. While my son thinks house plants are useless, and I used to care them to death, I have come to love them in recent years. Like my cats, they are something like children to me—definitely cheaper, definitely less work, yet work nevertheless, and a lot of pleasure.

I am pleased when my plants grow stronger; sometimes I talk to them—I love watching them grow a new leaf or new blooms. I get especially excited when one of my orchids begins to sprout a new flower stem, which then grows and unfolds over weeks, and blooms for months.

Plants add softness and life to a home, a calming and quiet living presence. Plants eliminate toxins from the air, absorb our carbon dioxide while emitting oxygen, and humidify the air by releasing water; their presence seems to increase productivity in offices and add to our well-being in general (apparently, sick people get well faster if they are around plants). From a decorative perspective, plants can make a statement, such as a tall ficus tree in a big space, little succulents growing between pebbles in a pretty pot, or a basket planted with a variety of plants. Plants add to the quality of life in so many ways.

Grasshopper or ant?   February 3, 2016

You may remember LaFontaine's fable of the ant that strategically planned its food reserves during the summer in preparation for winter, and the playful grasshopper who ended up without food because it played all summer long.

Shortcuts don't always work, and it often takes hindsight to realize it. We have taken many shortcuts on environmental and agricultural issues in favor of quick monetary gain. Whether through fracking, pesticides, factory farming, or a host of other quagmires, the money comes quick, but then. . .there is always, always, always, an ugly hidden cost, and in the end it costs much more.

Take the recent dramatic drop in oil and gas prices, which almost immediately led to people buying fewer electric and fuel-efficient cars. While buying that less-expensive vehicle right now, deferring getting those solar panels or better insulated windows, or delaying insulating your house may indeed save you money this year, the long-term consequences are no savings. Take the purchase of solar panels, for example. Payback is around six to eight years. That means that, after six to eight years, your electricity will be free for the life of the panels, which is around twenty or so years. So you get twelve years of free electricity! And keep in mind that the cost of electricity keeps going up. In addition, you are helping to cut down on the pollution caused by burning fossil fuels, which contributes to the warming of our planet. Win–win for all.

The hook? It requires an investment and a short-term material sacrifice in favor of long-term environmental and monetary gain. What's so bad about that? You do the same for retirement. You sacrifice something now for gain down the road.

Think like the ant: Think long-term!

Foraging 101 June 7, 2016

For the past few weeks I have had an abundant supply of wild greens in my backyard. Lambs quarters and dandelions are growing with abandon. Both can be eaten raw as salad greens, used in a smoothie, or quickly sautéed or steamed with some garlic, olive oil, and a squeeze of lemon. Dandelion leaves become bitter as the leaves grow bigger and older, so harvest the smaller ones if you don't like bitter greens. The yellow flowers are edible and look very pretty in a salad, or you can put them in your smoothie. Lambs quarter is a mild-tasting green and can be substituted in any recipe that calls for spinach or chard.

In a few weeks we are looking forward to a bumper crop of blackcaps. What's growing in your backyard?

Learning to lose July 12, 2016

It is time to move aside and consider the rest of our planet's inhabitants. It is time to shrink our economies. It is time to leave some of Nature unraped. British philosopher Alan Watts wrote: "a permanently victorious species destroys, not only itself, but all other life in its environment."

We depend on all other life on this planet. Without trees for oxygen, without plants for food, without wood and fiber for building and clothing, without water for drinking, without the animal kingdom for balance of our ecosystems, we do not exist.

We have already destroyed so much of life on Earth, let's not keep winning to the bitter end.

No waste   March 28, 2017

Nature leaves no waste, only people do. Nature's waste is sustainable because its decomposition follows a sustainable cycle in which every part feeds the next step in the cycle endlessly—animal waste and dead plant material compost back into the soil; carrion-eating birds and little critters take care of animal carcasses; trees absorb the carbon dioxide that animals and humans exhale. It is only us humans who have devised production processes that transform natural materials into stuff that is either itself not recyclable (think plastics) and creates trash that way, or whose manufacturing produces side effects in the form of waste and pollution (any industrial process).

Worldwide many towns and cities strive to become zero-waste by 2020. The goal of zero-waste is to recycle and compost everything so nothing goes into the landfill. It takes a strong commitment from the city, and a persistent education effort, to overcome people's initial resistance and learning curve. Take a look at your household trash and recycling logistics.

Can you do better? Since Nature leaves no waste let's remember that we, actually, are Nature, too.

White Man to Green Man   August 8, 2017

There was so much symbolism, albeit subconscious, in what my daughter said at lunchtime as we sat outside, looking at our faded-to-almost-white plaster cast of the Green Man. She said, "The white man needs to become the green man again," simply meaning we ought to give him a fresh coat of green stain.

Today's *New York Times* article about a draft report by federal agencies that we are already experiencing climate change here in the U.S.—that human activities are the primary culprit, and that temperatures have risen dramatically since 1980—reminds us how interwoven with Nature we really are, we can't escape it.

It is high time that we White men return from feeling superior to Nature to respecting it, working with it, recognizing that we humans are Nature too, and cannot exist without it. Nature is what surrounds us, provides us with everything we need to live—food to nourish ourselves, fiber to clothe ourselves, building materials, plants for medicine to heal ourselves, and materials to express ourselves creatively via music and the visual arts.

The Green Man is an ancient, mostly Celtic, symbol for man's symbiosis with Nature. While indigenous cultures have steadfastly maintained their intertwined relationship with Nature, as much they were able to through the long assault period by Western culture, we whites completely forgot that we are Nature, that we owe everything to it, that we cannot live without it.

May the White Man become the Green Man again.

Barefooting it   August 22, 2017

I forgot about walking barefoot. My kids walk around the house barefoot all the time. And my sister reminded me when she came to visit recently. Walking barefoot frees the feet of their unnatural shoesy confines. Walking barefoot is grounding.

Walking barefoot outside is even more grounding. Grounding techniques do just that—connecting us to the ground in order to rebalance the mind and reconnect us with the Earth. In addition, walking barefoot outdoors—on grass, sand, or even more adventurous ground—lets us absorb negative ions. Negative ions counter all the positive ions electronics spew out (Himalayan salt lamps also generate negative ions and counter the effects of electronics).

So, take your shoes and socks off while the weather is warm, and go for a barefoot walk outside. As little as five minutes a day is beneficial.

Contemplations on our
relationship with animals

The best cat food   April 11, 2012

Yesterday was cat food day again, which happens once a month at our house. "Garbage in, garbage out," or the flip side. "quality food in, health out," is a motto that works for us as it does for animals. Our older three-year-old tomcat was raised on "high quality" dry food—out of ignorance. Well, the consequences began to show last year. He had gained weight and had become lethargic. So, besides getting him an adorable little black female companion from the shelter, I researched cat food.

Since then I have been making my own from scratch based on a recipe by vet Lisa Pierson. It is a mix of raw and semi-cooked chicken, gizzards, livers, and various supplements. The results speak louder than words. Within three months our cat had naturally slimmed down and regained his vitality. Both cats have shimmery, shiny fur, chase each other through the house, and maintain an ideal weight. Our holistic vet confirmed that making your own cat food "is the best thing you can do for your cats."

Buzzing bees   April 17, 2012

Our new bees arrived this past weekend. The day they arrived one of them got caught in my hair when it explored the garden. I panicked and tried to whip it out of my hair—wrong thing to do. Bees don't like sudden movements. So the poor thing stung me (and lost its life, which I felt really badly about). But that's not what this post is about.

What it is about is this—yesterday I was in and out of the garden many times, hanging up laundry. Each time I came outside two or three bees soon enough buzzed around me. Maybe they wanted to warn me not to come too close to their new home, maybe they only wanted to check me out (my bee language skills are not that good yet). This time I moved very slowly in awareness of the bees. I talked to them (I told them that I wasn't going to harm them) and let them "sniff me out" without any sudden movements. And I passed the test without getting stung.

Don't think I am crazy when I am trying to convey that I attempted to communicate with the bees. I am currently reading Martha Beck's new book *Finding Your Way in a Wild New World*, about consciousness and how to operate within that non-material plane. Check it out. That is the plane from which we can communicate with animals, that is what I was trying to do with the bees—the second time around.

Poor bees   *April 9, 2013*

Whether Einstein really said that mankind would perish within four years if all the bees died is less important than the realization that bees are crucially important to our food chain, and they are indeed dying at an alarming rate. It is, however, true that Rudolf Steiner predicted a hundred years ago, that the bee population would be damaged or might die out if we kept raising and treating the bees in an industrial way—and this is exactly what is happening right now. It is also a fact that our crops will decline by about forty percent if the bees die out because there are not enough other pollinators out there.

While big-ag farmers and big-ag beekeepers still talk about the "mysterious" colony collapse syndrome, and some scientists still remain vague about the cause ("it's the mites"—no, the bees' genetic make-up is weak and they can't stand up to the mites any longer!), the cause is eminently clear to holistic beekeepers and all who are in tune with Nature. The bees' genetics and immune systems have been weakened by the industrial approach to both beekeeping and farming. Monocultures deprive the bees of variety in their food, the poor things feed on a diet of poisons (all the –icides we spray on crops and gardens), industrial beekeepers take their honey away and feed them diluted sugar water instead, and they wake them up in February from their winter slumber, pack the hives by the hundreds onto trucks, and shuttle them up the coast to a different orchard every six weeks. This treatment is worse than what peasants endured in the Middle Ages. No wonder the bees die of mistreatment and weakness.

What to do? It is so encouraging that backyard and rooftop bee-keeping is becoming so popular. It is also very encouraging that more women, who are naturally more nurturing, are becoming bee-keepers. But you don't have to become a beekeeper to help the situation. Just stop spraying your lawn (what's wrong with dandelions and clover? the bees love them), stop spraying your roses (find more natural and gentle ways to interact with your garden), buy more organic produce, and simply become more informed.

Shark fin soup and hope   July 1, 2013

If the Chinese are back-peddling on shark fin soup, so ubiquitous at all festive banquets of the past, there is hope for changes in our attitude about a lot of other things as well. I am thinking of idling stances on such pressing issues as climate change, pollution, animal welfare, GMOs, child prostitution, and many other ugly realities. It seems to me that ultimately our collective indecisiveness on these issues boils down to the hesitance of wrestling ourselves away from the profit-first model.

If we only realized that the well-being-first model benefits us all around. Bonnie Tsui wrote in the *Times* about the changing attitude of the Chinese on serving shark fin soup at important banquets, previously a sign of "honoring (and impressing) your guest." I was served shark fin soup at several banquets in my company's honor in the late 1980s, when we lived in Hong Kong, and was oblivious of the gruesome practice (which I can't bear to describe here, but you can look it up).

Because it has been such an inherent component of Chinese food culture, I was really quite amazed to read that, "Last summer, the Chinese government announced that it would stop serving the dish at official state banquets." Here's to change for the better, change towards well-being, change towards respect of Nature and all living beings.

Animal consciousness   July 9, 2013

I have always wanted to delve a bit deeper into the question of animal consciousness. The death of our dear cat Snowball a few weeks ago became the catalyst for it. We all know the relationship between brain size and depth of consciousness, awareness, and intelligence. So it might seem that the larger the animal's brain, the deeper a relationship we can forge with it because of the animal's deeper awareness. I had never experienced an animal relationship until we got Snowball, our first cat (I grew up in city apartments with fish and hamsters—no deep relationships there). He was white, with a few well-placed black spots, gentle and regal, and sociable to a point. Sometimes, he would jump up on the bed to snuggle, but he was not a lap cat.

A few years later we adopted Mieze as a companion for him, our little black, very assertive female tuxedo cat. She talks a lot, while Snowball did not, she jumps on our laps as he did not, she'll wake us up in the morning by prancing around on the headboard and meowing by the side of the bed (not out of hunger, but for companionship). She is very sprite, quick, and playful, a perfect hunter (she even caught bats that had made their way into the house on two occasions); he'd lost a lot of his playfulness over the years. I learned how individual animals' personalities are, and how they truly become a beloved family member. Just as with my children, my nurturing gene kicked in, and I make sure the cats get the best holistic cat food and vet care and emotional nurturing.

Yet René Descartes, the 17th-century French philosopher, believed that animals were nothing more than mechanized, soulless, feelingless, rightless moving bodies we have dominion over—a prevailing understanding of his times. And you wonder about many still prevailing animal practices, like dog and cock and bull fights, raising animals for fur, CAFOs (concentrated animal feeding operations), selectively breeding food animals so abnormally that they cannot function anymore (chickens with breasts so heavy they tip over, corn fed cows whose intestines scream because the diet is so unsuitable to their digestive systems, etc.).

We have come a long way thanks to animal rights groups and wake-up calls that happen spontaneously when we look an animal in the eyes and see a soul or consciousness staring back at us with meaning. Coming to the end of reading *Cat Body, Cat Mind* by vet Dr. Michael Fox, who obviously has a deeply spiritual understanding of life, I regret not having shown our Mieze the dead body of her companion Snowball.

Animals seem to understand the passing of close mates and companions, and need closure like we do.

Now we are working on integrating her new companion, Peter Pepper, into our household. Fox says that it is important for animals to have a like companion so they always remember who they are. We had found Snowball on the side of the road when he was four or five weeks old, and we are not sure he ever totally understood how to act among cats. Maybe he was always a bit more human than cat.

I am still intrigued and would like to learn more about this collective animal consciousness I read about, that bees or cats or cows are not as individuated as we humans, and are more a fragment of a larger encompassing cat consciousness, or bee consciousness, or cow consciousness. It may shed some light on our own embeddedness in a larger collective human or universal consciousness, how inseparable we really are of the greater collective consciousness.

Animals in our life   December 6, 2013

Since the death of our beloved cat this past summer I have been pondering our relationships with animals in general, and more specifically my relationship with our cats. I have read several books on communication with animals since then, because I really see a soul when I look into an animal's eyes (a cow's on a walk, a deer's in a field, a lion's in a zoo, a horse's in a stable), the same way we see it in people —you have probably heard the saying, "The eyes are the mirror of the soul." Well, it's as true for animals as it is for humans (and why would it be different anyhow?).

It is telling to watch people interacting with their pets. Amelia Kinkade, the noted animal communicator, writes in her book *The Language of Miracles,* "The animals are here to facilitate our enlightenment through their unconditional love." Some people get it, some not so much yet.

While I by no means pretend to be able to communicate with our cats, I totally get that you can tune into them by becoming silent (quieting the mind, as in meditation, or simply tuning in and tuning other stuff out) and learning it the way we would learn Spanish or Russian. It is a matter of practicing and applying the appropriate techniques. You wouldn't try to learn to speak Spanish by practicing scales or chopping up onions.

What astonished me most from reading this particular book is how well developed animals' emotional lives are, and how precisely they are able to communicate to anyone who is able to listen on how they are being treated, on what they prefer to eat, on their own and even their owner's state of health, on their preferred toys, on the layout of the place where they live, on the family dynamics of their host family, even everyone's names. Quite amazing.

I am so much more careful now with how I interact with the cats after reading this book because I realize that they are more aware than you would ever believe—a total eye-opener.

Piranhas and the eco-mind   January 6, 2014

It is interesting and eye-opening to realize how "the truth" can be so deeply in the eyes of the beholder. We see what we believe, and we don't see what we don't believe. We have been thinking along the (somewhat) misinterpreted Darwinian lines of Nature's potential ferociousness and cruelty in the name of the survival of the fittest. But scientists are beginning to dismantle this paradigm. Sunday's *New York Times* article took wildly exaggerated reports about the supposedly bloodthirsty piranhas apart and reduced them to nothing much. Growing up, I remember hearing stories about entire cows supposedly being stripped to the bones in minutes by a huge swarm of these little fish. But I also acknowledge reading later about indigenous people wading and swimming fearlessly in piranha-inhabited waters.

A short video on Suzanne Simard's work on the wood-wide-web and the mycorhizzal (mushroom) network recently made the rounds on Facebook. Dr. Simard is involved in research about mother trees (huge old trees in the woods) and their social network, where plant seedlings grow up around the mother tree, and mushroom networks reach far underground, living in symbiotically nourishing relationships with the trees for their mutual benefit.

Nature is becoming friendlier by the minute as our outlook on the environment is shifting and we are becoming more eco-minded.

Spiritual cats   February 7, 2014

Would you believe that I communicated with our three cats (two alive, one dead) telepathically through an intermediary? Some people, and a few family members are among them, will say that this is a bunch of hogwash. But I live my life on the spiritual side (with a good dose of critical-analytical thinking!), and I am always looking for deeper ways to understand and connect with the world. So I am open to something like this and don't dismiss it simply because it goes against the present scientific-material paradigm.

Among other questions we had been curious about the premature (in our view) death of our beloved first cat Snowball, and the jumpiness of our third cat Peter Pepper. I had recently read that it is possibly to communicate with animals telepathically. So when a friend told me about someone right in town (though distance is irrelevant) who has this ability, I jumped at the opportunity.

I was amazed by how much these animals understand (be careful how you treat them, and what you say in front of them!), and at the depth of their spirituality. Snowball responded to our question about his early death at age five that a life ought not to be judged by how short or long it was but by what was accomplished, that it was an immense privilege for him to have opened the whole family's awareness to the animal kingdom, and that his five years with us were very meaningful for him.

Peter Pepper, another little sage, communicated that he was aware of his eye condition, which I had asked about, that he resonates with the sound of Tibetan prayer bowls (boy, where did that come from?), and that that would help him heal his condition. This was quite coincidental, as I had become aware of a Tibetan prayer bowl iPhone meditation app just a week or so earlier. Hm. . . .

Make of it what you wish, but the answers of our three cats had enormous meaning for us.

In awe   *July 14, 2014*

I am always in total awe when I see big creatures out there in the wild. Seeing a bear (two days ago at lunchtime out my office window), a fox (same thing, out my office window), even a deer, a flock of turkeys, or a moose (last year in Alaska), seems not only exotic to me, but twists my reality back into place. These magnificent creatures show me how awesome Nature is, that we must respect their magnitude, their sheer force and power. There is always a bit of incredulity at their sight, maybe feeling privileged that they show themselves, and awe that we are part of the same environment that sustains them too.

It touches something deep down in me.

Octopus consciousness   *January 15, 2016*

Many scientists still do not feel comfortable attributing some sort of cognition to animals. But all of us dog and cat lovers simply *know* that our beloved pets have a consciousness, albeit different from ours. They recognize different people, know our character (whether we are kind to them or not), can make themselves understood (being bored, being hungry, hurting), and exhibit feelings (mourning when a close mate has died, or exuberance when you take your dog out to run on a beautiful day). My daughter says her Betta fish watches her as she moves about her room.

Maybe Paul the Octopus, who supposedly predicted many FIFA World Cup outcomes correctly, was instrumental in spreading the idea of octopuses' intelligence to the wider public. I am currently reading Sy Montgomery's delightful new book *The Soul of an Octopus*. It is quite amazing to find out that these animals, whose beingness seems so much further removed from ours than even cats or dogs, recognize their keepers and distinguish between people they like (reaching out and tasting their skin with their suction cups—yes, they taste with their suction cups, and who knows what they are able to taste, hormones? medication in the blood stream? feelings?) and dislike (they'll squirt those with water).

Octopuses are enormously intelligent and inquisitive, and

have been known to exit their supposedly tightly secured tanks to go exploring. They can go through extreme appearance changes in a matter of seconds, not only to blend in to their environment to protect against predators, but also to express their disposition, such as white and smooth when calm, or red and bumpy when excited. Each octopus has a distinct character.

It seems to me that we are slowly entering a new and more inclusive era of understanding the Nature that surrounds us —my daughter is into crystals and swears she can feel them pulsating.

How you treat animals   May 17, 2016

More of us need to know how the majority of animals raised for human consumption are treated—it's dreadful, and maybe this term isn't even strong enough (read Jonathan Safran Foer's *Eating Animals* if you really want to know more). It also says something about us that pharmaceuticals are tested on animals kept in captivity and subjected to potentially harmful side effects. And that kill shelters exist is a horror. Betta fish are routinely kept in solitary confinement in minuscule bubble tanks. Thank goodness big game hunting is on its way out, the ivory trade also (they kill the whole huge elephant just for the tusks, and don't even bother to eat the meat), at least almost, and shark fin soup popularity is down. But people still wear fur coats, and the Chinese still illegally trade animal parts they believe have healing properties. Nevertheless, zoos treat animals much better nowadays than, say, a hundred years ago, providing them with habitats that resemble the places they came from, diets as close to their natural diets as possible, and offer them distraction and exercise.

I believe that we are unable to harm an animal once we look it deeply in the eyes—because then we connect with its soul. When animals are kept in pens under anonymous conditions we don't connect with each one individually. That's why people have no qualms about eating supermarket meat. If we all had to look our steak in the eyes, work in a kill shelter, spend a week in a slaughterhouse or a pharmaceutical animal testing lab, things would change very, very quickly.

Poor bats   June 17, 2016

Our bat house is an important conversation piece even though it is still uninhabited.

Bats are in as dire a straight these days as bees. Many of them have died off due to white-nose syndrome (a fungal disease), while bees have succumbed to colony collapse syndrome en masse. Bats are important insect population regulators and can eat their weight in mosquitos and other insects on a daily basis (wow, I would need to eat one hundred thirty pounds of food each day). We like to give afflictions fancy names. But what is the real cause behind these massive die-offs?

Why do we humans become so sick in later life with cancer, diabetes, arthritis, or heart disease? Many signs point to diet, toxins, and a stressful, unnatural lifestyle. Studies into white-nose and colony collapse syndrome have also indicated that toxins, aka pesticides, aka neonicotinoids, may weaken these small creatures' tiny immune systems. Our toxic agricultural practices are upsetting the apple cart, aka ecosystem balance. Not only is it likely that our pollinators and insect population regulators are dying for those reasons, but their die-offs are causing further ecosystem imbalances down the line because we'll have trouble pollinating our produce, and the insect population will grow out of whack (watch out for Zika and West Nile).

Luckily many bats live in the cliff next to us. Bats flutter around at dusk on warm summer nights, when most birds have settled down for the night. Have you seen any bats lately?

Unconditional love   March 7, 2017

Why do we love our pets so much? Or why do we love animals in general so much? Look in the eyes of an animal—a wolf, a fox, or a raccoon. I think we love animals so much because of their unconditional love. Animals have no hidden agenda.

Wild animals may not show their love in the way our pets do; nevertheless their eyes convey a genuineness, a certain innocence, a truthfulness, a vulnerability, a transparency we admire because we don't necessarily see it in ourselves and our fellow wo/men. We humans are so much more complicated. We interpret, we judge, we evaluate, we question, we wonder, we manipulate, we doubt.

Why can't we be a bit more like animals?

Musings
on food and eating

Holistic living, artisanal cheese March 25, 2012

This blog is about holistic living, which for me is authentic living. Take the difference between processed cheese and artisanal raw milk cheese (or the difference between a Twinkie and a homemade oatmeal cookie). Raw milk cheese is authentic cheese, the way cheese was originally made from simple ingredients that came straight from Nature, while processed cheese is an industrial factory-made product that only emulates cheese. When I am talking about *authentic* living, it is about *deep* living, life with all its emotions, joys, and sorrows, life beyond material acquisitions and the rushing around from one activity to the next, a life true to who we are.

Life, to me, is about finding your true self through interaction with people and your environment. There is something deeply satisfying about spending quality time with friends and family, a satisfaction we can't quite recreate through the purchase of a new dress or earrings. Much has been written about living in the moment. When I cook, for example, I am so self-absorbed that I forget everything around me and am only aware of what I am making. That is when I truly live in the moment. That is deep living, or holistic living, or authentic living. It is meaningful and satisfying.

Why eat organic? September 7, 2012

The stale and narrow premise that organic food distinguishes itself from conventionally grown food simply by its nutritional content is on the table again in today's *Times* article by Kenneth Chang about a new meta-study to that effect. But, as Sonya Lunder, a senior analyst with the Environmental Working Group, stresses, many who buy organic food are aware of the complexity of the issues beyond the mere nutritional aspect.

The nutrition debate leaves, as in the past, a whole host of other reasons for why to buy organics off the table. Besides ingesting fewer residual toxins from pesticides, buying organic groceries, produce, meat, and fish means choosing the health of the environment and biodiversity over sprayed and mono-cultured fields; it means voting for the health of the farmworkers to protect them from exposure to toxic pesticides and herbicides; in the case of meat and farmed fish, it means choosing to avoid ingestion of antibiotics and surface bacteria; and it means voting against genetically modified plants and animals. Lastly, if buying from a nearby organic farm, your choice is linked to choosing local over global.

So, buying organics is a vote for a multitude of betterments, not simply a choice for more nutritious food.

Food, glorious food   May 21, 2013

Food is one of my favorite subjects because I grew up in food cultures. For me food counts as "entertainment," as going to a concert or the movies might for someone else. While foodies know that food is more than fuel, there is also more to food than the surprise of a clever new taste combination, or the goodness of a sun-ripened peach in August. Food provides us with energy in more ways than the obvious.

For one, there is the life energy we ingest with our food. It is most vibrant in freshly plucked and raw foods, and least vibrant in processed foods, because those are so far removed from their natural origins. With meat, one consideration is how the animal was raised and treated, what it ate, and how it found its end. This all finds its energetic way into our meal.

In addition, food feeds the soul when enjoyed in a harmonious atmosphere and in company. That kind of food experience literally nourishes us spiritually. And it sure doesn't have to be fancy to be meaningful. It can be a picnic, it can be an ethnic festivity, it can be a potluck, or an outdoor meal. It's more about the overall experience, what goes with it—friends, the setting, the conversation. *Bon appétit! Guten Appetit! Buon appetito!*

Fermented foods, good bacteria

May 31, 2013

Looks like the mainstream is coming around to the fact that microorganisms are not only all around us but also all over our insides, and that that's not necessarily a bad thing. As a matter of fact, we are realizing now that bacteria are necessary to our gut health and a strong immune system. Antibacterial soaps and wipes and sprays actually contribute to weakening our immune system because the lack of bacteria over-sensitizes the body and removes the chance to interact with our environment. And doctors are becoming much more cautious in prescribing antibiotics for human consumption (now we just need the meat industry to come on board and stop feeding the animals preventative antibiotics, trace elements of which remain in the meat, and also end up in the water cycle—so ultimately this practice bites us in the behind). The few times I was treated with antibiotics as a child, our pediatrician stressed the importance of eating yogurt every day to replenish the gut bacteria destroyed by the medication.

You may have read of the newest treatment for intestinal inflammation, fecal bacteriotherapy, which involves the deliberate injection of fecal bacteria from a healthy person to replenish a sick person's gut bacteria.

Turns out that most cultures have traditions of fermenting foods, foods that "turn" and develop lacto bacteria. When eaten regularly, fermented foods keep replenishing our gut fauna naturally, foods and drinks such as yogurt and kefir, cheese, sauerkraut and kimchi, pickled vegetables (not made with vinegar but naturally fermented), beer and wine, cured sausage, or sourdough bread. Consult Sally Fallon's anti-establishment cookbook *Nour-*

ishing Traditions on really easy recipes for fermented vegetables, as well as Sandor Ellix Katz's new fermented food bible *The Art of Fermentation.*

Keep eating (raw milk!) cheeses, cultured butter, and all those other delicious fermented foods.

Boring homogenous food   October 15, 2013

I love food, I love to travel, and I love to try food from other places in the world. Bill Clinton said, "We need to look at how people do things in other places." Of course he did not say that with regard to food. He said it at a sustainability conference about expanding our insular and one-sided perspective here in the U.S. on politics, energy policy, and sustainability. But the idea is the same. Fast food joints turn out the same food, whether you are in Paris, Los Angeles, or New York. Whether in food or Western culture at large, homogenization simply goes against Nature's grain, because Nature is all about diversity and increasing complexity with ongoing development. And what we eat depends on what grows where we live. Different soil, different climate, different culture, different ecosystems all create different foods, which in turn allow us to create completely different dishes.

What fear of life let us be comforted by the knowledge that we can eat the same hamburger and french fries even if we travel halfway around the globe? I will scream if one more pizza joint, one more Italian restaurant or Chinese take-out, opens in our town. Instead, give me Indian, Thai, a fish restaurant, real Chinese, or true local American.

It's about discovery; it's about opening up to new tastes, new experiences, new ingredients, a zest for life and all it has to offer. I tried duck tongues (tough and chewy) and chicken feet (didn't like those) in China, green papaya salad in the Philippines (delicious), cherimoyas in Peru (creamily yummy), jackfruit in Hong

Kong (so-so; ripe ones are so smelly they are forbidden on the Singapore subway), and frog legs and *escargots* in France (love them).

Let's celebrate the diversity of life; let's discover what people have to say in other places, how they eat in other places, how they do things differently from us. Why must we be politically correct? Why can't we live with our differences and appreciate them? Discuss them? Learn from them? The entire world cannot be homogenous.

Imagine if the whole country were Republican? Or Democrat? If everyone wore the same outfit? Boring.

Food as fuel?   November 19, 2013

According to the scientific and mechanistic worldview this culture has subscribed to for the past three hundred or so years, food is not much more than fuel in form of calories that can be described on a nutritional label in terms of its scientific components. How sad and simplistic! How unromantic and incomplete!

According to the holistic model, food is nourishment for body and spirit in so many ways. According to this model, quality is at least as important as quantification. It matters what you eat, it matters in what circumstances and company you eat, it matters how your food was grown or raised, it matters whether your food is fresh or processed, it matters whether you enjoy your food or not, it matters how you relate to it. It becomes a complex and multi-faceted approach.

Guess which model is more fun, more enjoyable, more meaningful, and ultimately healthier?

Feel your body, understand food   July 18, 2014

Have you ever gotten up from the table and felt sluggish and stuffed, or perhaps even lethargic after a meal? Has it happened that you've eaten something and then felt your stomach acting up an hour or so later? On the other hand, have you noticed that certain foods energize you, and that your stomach feels light after eating, yet satisfied?

I always yearn for lots of greens, raw or sautéed, and my stomach feels light after I eat them. When I eat meat in larger quantities on the other hand, my stomach feels heavy and full. My husband says that cheese and wheat clog him up.

You can learn to tune in to your body and understand which foods are beneficial for your particular digestive system. Science wished there were a one-kind-fits-all diet. But that is just not so. Nature is complex, and we are complex. Think of extreme diets like that of the Masaai in Africa (beef, blood, milk), or the Inuit diet that consists mostly of fish and other marine protein. These peoples' stomachs would rebel if prescribed the Mediterranean diet. Yet, the Mediterranean diet has been touted as the world's healthiest. I like it very much, but I come from Northern Europe, and rye bread, sauerkraut, and butter all work well for my system, too. Or how about the raw food diet (just another craze—some of us may just need a balanced mix of raw and cooked foods), or the Paleo diet, which often has been misconstrued as encompassing lots of meat (hunter-gatherers ate little meat and only perennial plants since there was no agriculture yet, ergo no annual grains). And let's not forget veganism (beware—especially in childhood and adolescence we need protein to develop the brain).

It helps to understand your ethnic heritage, which can be a bit of challenge in this country when your heritage is often something exotic like Irish-Italian, or Japanese-Spanish. Our digestive systems tune into the plants and animals in our particular geographic area over hundreds and even thousands of years. I have even read that our digestive systems haven't yet fully adapted to the annual grains our agriculture of the past ten thousand years has brought forth.

So lean in to your body, tune in, learn to read your digestive system's signals—good and bad—and let them tell you a story of what works for you, what makes you feel good, and what energizes you.

Oh, those late summer tomatoes   August 22, 2014

There is nothing better than a sweet, tree-ripened peach, a sun-ripened, soft and warm tomato that's just been plucked, or springy and perky greens that were harvested in the early morning hours before the sun comes up. Just-harvested produce, which has sun ripened to perfection, has so much life force. You can taste all the minerals and sunny goodness.

We lose those characteristics when we buy produce at the supermarket. Supermarket produce gets harvested before it ripens, so it can be transported safely over long distances and is "ready" when it finally arrives at the store. That works more or less well for some produce types but not for others. Bananas and tomatoes can be harvested while still green and will keep ripening on the windowsill, although they will not acquire that naturally ripened sweetness. A hard supermarket peach or plum, on the other hand, will never get that juicily delicious sweet taste a sun-ripened fruit naturally has—refrigerated, prematurely picked peaches usually turn mealy, and the plums stay sourish.

That's why it is so rewarding to buy produce locally when it is in season. So what if you can only have strawberries in June and July? The local kind tastes ten times better than the spongy clamshell strawberries that come from far away year round. In Germany there is the annual spring asparagus craze that lasts for about six weeks, when the fat white stalks are ready. Here, I love the big juicy tomatoes that are at their best in late August and early September, when the sun has had enough time to deepen their color to a profound red and they almost taste as sweet as candy.

Calories, not real nourishment   September 24, 2014

"We can buy calories," wrote Charles Eisenstein, "but not real nourishment." Gaining nourishment from food is a many-layered process that includes a lot more than counting the calories of a meal or dissecting its nutritional content. Those are quantifying analyses. But the soul also gets nourishment from the qualitative aspects in and around food.

The first thing that comes to mind has to do with how the food grew, was or was not processed, and how it was made. Vegetables and fruits grown in healthy and mineral-rich soil on a small farm with loving care, grown without -cides (pesti-, insecti-, fungi-), harvested at the height of their ripeness or readiness, and cooked as soon as possible after harvesting, are incredibly nourishing for body and soul. Their intrinsic quality is so much more complex than produce that was harvested before ripening (bananas, peaches, tomatoes grown on large farms, all get harvested before their prime to ensure unsquooshed arrival at the supermarket), had to be shuttled cross country or across continents, and then sits in the supermarket for another few days before making it to our fridge, where it sits yet another few days. Same goes for meat (for those who do eat meat). It matters in what surroundings the animal was kept, how it was handled, what it was fed, and how it met its end. That quality, which we introduce into our body, has an influence on our spirit.

Other elements that add a more ethereal quality to the food we eat are the care and love and interest with which we prepare and cook the food. A lovingly prepared and composed dish will have a better energetic quality than a quickly slapped together microwaved meal. Your homemade jar of jam has so much more qualitative depth than the one from the supermarket that was made industrially.

Lastly, the context in which we eat a meal can nourish the soul. A nicely set table helps; taking the time to sit down for a family meal creates a comforting and warm tone of togetherness at the end of the day; and sharing a leisurely meal with friends imbues the food with a different meaning than eating alone. And just think of those special holiday meals coming up soon.

Less (food) waste   December 30, 2014

We are not always aware of the abundance we live in, and grateful and thankful for it. As a result we create a lot of waste, personally and as a culture. This is the first of several blog posts on becoming more aware of the abundance that surrounds us, and at the same time reducing waste in different areas of our lives.

Why waste reduction? When we respect something, when we are truly appreciative of it, then we handle it with a certain reverence and wouldn't carelessly throw it away. That goes for food as it does for other things in life. Sometimes one of my kids will come home and put their school sandwich back in the fridge. Now what? I have at times repackaged it the next day, but often end up eating it myself so it doesn't go to waste. When my son was much, much younger he threw out a perfectly good (wrapped) sandwich he did not care for. I was so incensed that I made him take it out of the trash and eat it—he still talks about it.

With a bit more reverence for all the food we have (just today it struck me at the supermarket how much food we have access to so easily, what abundance!), let's try to reduce food waste, the first of the wastes I will be addressing.

One rule is to be a good leftovers processor—eat them, freeze them, or cook them up with something new, but don't let them go bad. I save leftover bread pieces in the freezer until I have enough to make a sweet or savory breakfast strata. My mom makes a "tapas meal" every so often with all the little frozen leftover dishes. If you do buy produce in bulk, like I do, process those vegetables you can't eat right away by blanching and freezing them as meal building blocks for later use, or cooking them up in a soup or stew to be frozen. If food does go bad in your fridge, buy less or space your supermarket trips further apart. And how about going through your fridge once a week and either making a meal from all the leftovers right then or freezing what you can't use immediately?

We have so much, let's be grateful for it.

Tasting soil and climate   February 6, 2015

As our culture becomes increasingly interested, sophisticated, and educated in all things food, you may stumble upon the word *terroir* on this side of the Atlantic. It is a typically French term connected to that country's deep and intense food culture. The idea behind fast food is the exact opposite of what *terroir* expresses. Fast food companies want to assure you of the exact same hamburger or french fries taste regardless of whether you buy them in Beijing, Moscow, Los Angeles, or Buenos Aires—worldwide uniformity of taste. *Terroir*, on the contrary, celebrates the unique combination of local soil and climate conditions in a particular area, and how they influence the taste of the foods grown there.

Terroir is perhaps easiest to understand in connection with wine because we know from experience that the same grape type, say a Chardonnay, grown in different geographical places will yield very different-tasting wines. That is the reason why the French don't label their wines by grape type, as we do here, but by provenance, such as Château Lafite, or Saint-Aubin, or Domaine Sylvain Langoureau, which of course requires a vastly larger knowledge base.

Beyond wine, we have come to be aware of *terroir* influence on food as it relates to chocolate (Trader Joe's offers a chocolate passport that features small chocolate samples from eight different cocoa bean growing countries in the world), honey (depends on the type of flower nectar collected), and single-malt whiskeys (depends a lot on the local water). But *terroir* also comes out in the taste of meat. The Spanish Jamón Ibérico, for example, is prized for its particular taste that comes from the black pigs' natural diet of grass, herbs, and acorns, specific to that region in southern Spain.

Locally, I have bought organic chickens from two different farmers. Both taste and texture of the meat, and even the shape of the chickens, were vastly different, even though the two farms are not even twenty miles apart. Coffee connoisseurs always say that water can make or break a good cup of coffee. City water usually has added chlorine, and often also fluoride, which alter the taste of the water, while local well water tastes different from one well to the next, depending on its particular mineral content.

Local food is so much more complex and exciting! Happy tasting!

Celebrating the beauty of food   February 13, 2015

In case you hadn't guessed it yet, I love food. Food is so important in my life that I also decorate the house with it. Not all over, of course (no apple basket in the bedroom, or kiwi display in the bathroom). I mean in the living-dining-kitchen area, where we are inspired to eat it or cook with it (and won't forget about it).

When I return with lots and lots and lots of produce from our once-a-month food co-op delivery, or from a trip to Trader Joe's to get my organic in-between-deliveries fruit, I pile it up in bowls and on platters, and display it on countertops and tables. I play with the colors of the produce and match, complement, or juxtapose it with the colors of the vessels. The yellow leopard bowl goes well with the yellow of the bananas and the muted green avocados; I like the linear cardboard container the brownish-reddish kumato tomatoes lie in like peas in a pod just the way it is; and I picked the silver bowl this week for apples and kiwis to sit next to the silver candle holders.

Especially now, towards the end of winter, when we are beginning to crave color but are still a month away from the spring bulb flowers, produce colors look gorgeous. Don't hide it in the fridge— play with it, display it, celebrate and enjoy it.

Grass fed is best   April 7, 2015

I used to think that the most important improvement to our dairy consumption would to buy organic milk, butter, and cheese, what with the growth hormones and antibiotics they feed the cows these days (and that make it into our body and into the groundwater). But I have had to adjust my thinking.

Buying organic butter, and cheese, and milk only assures that the cows were fed an organic (grain—gulp) diet (which is unhealthy for the poor animals and makes them sick). That meat from grass fed cows (their natural diet) is healthier for us than from grain fed or grain finished cows, has gradually trickled into mainstream awareness (less fat, more healthy Omega-3, higher in various other micronutrients).

But the same is also of course true for milk, cheese, and butter from grass-fed cows—much higher levels of vitamin K2 and Omega-3 fatty acids, which actually promote heart health (yes, eat more of it!). Studies have shown that countries where cows are mostly grass fed (Ireland, Australia) have much lower levels of heart disease!

Organic butter really does not buy you much; butter from grass fed cows does.

Live foods/dead foods   June 12, 2015

I am currently researching *live* foods—and *dead* foods—in juxtaposition. A lot of what you find at your local supermarket is dead food. Food that's been manufactured (funny way to talk about food, no?) in a factory (yep, that's where breakfast cereal comes from, or processed cheese, or bottled dressing) has no life energy.

Dead food is basically any food that comes in a container and is sold in the center aisles of your supermarket. Food advocates have long recommended shopping the *perimeter* of your supermarket in order to eat better, because that's where produce, fish and meat, bread, and dairy are sold—although even supermarket meat (and fish), and supermarket dairy and breads, are adulterated (which is a whole other chapter).

So what are live foods? Food is created through a transformational process of sunlight into energy—photosynthesis. A raw green plant grown above ground is just about as live a food as you can get, as its relationship with the sun is so direct. So,, salad in other words, leafy greens, and anything raw; hence the recent craze over the Raw Food Movement.

A tub of *I Can't Believe It's Not Butter*, or *Cheez Whizz*, or *Funny Frosting* in a tub on the other hand, is just about as far away from sunlight energy as you can possibly get—zero, empty calories, no minerals and vitamins for sure. The further removed from sunlight a food is, the less life energy it has. Meat is two steps removed from sunlight—the animal eats grass, which grew with the help of sunlight. Meat from predators is yet further removed from sun energy, which may well be the reason why humans don't usually eat it (there are some exceptions with some indigenous tribes, as far as I know). Lion steak, anyone?

Some of the alivest (is this a word?) food is sprouts, and leafy greens have more direct life energy than, for example, root vegetables. Have you ever thought about the fact that some of the largest animals on this planet are plant eaters? Elephants, rhinos, cattle, hippos, dinosaurs (the largest of them all) are all greens eaters, whether grass or leaves. Wheatgrass and barley grass juice are some of the most healing potions you can ingest.

Take a look at what you currently eat and consider adding more greens and more raw foods to your diet. It will increase your energy level.

This or that? April 28, 2015

Processed cheese slice with yellow dye #5 or raw milk artisanal cheese from a small farm?

Canteloupe melons tasting like cardboard or freshly plucked cherry tomatoes bursting with sun ripened flavor?

Cornfed, antibiotic-supplemented, growth hormone-infested beef from a feedlot cow with red dye #3 to make it look fresh or perhaps no meat at all?

This or that?

Going Paleo? June 2, 2015

Is the Paleo diet another one of those diet fads like the Atkins diet or the South Beach diet? Come to think of it, there may be a bit more to it. The so-called Western diet, which is now traveling east and infecting Europe, India, and China, is full of sugar and starches. Given that starches in the form of grains, and transformed into bread, pasta, pizza, and cereals—our new daily staples—have only been in our diet since the advent of agriculture about ten thousand years ago, they seem to throw our million-and-some-year-old digestive systems for a loop. Add to the starches the addicting amounts of sugar we seem powerless to control, because big food puts them into everything from pickles (why?) and mustard, mayonnaise (seriously?) and bread (what's it doing in there?), to pasta sauce, breakfast cereals, soft drinks, and whatever else they can find, you may be in for a health mess unless you cook everything from scratch. And the health mess shows. Celiac disease, diabetes, rheumatoid arthritis, gluten sensitivity in general, perhaps even cancer, all seem to point to the same evil, sugar and grains, and are on a drastic rise.

I admit that I used to boast that my digestive system could handle all that grain, and what was it with all those gluten-intolerant people. After all, I grew up in the land of baguettes and croissants, and was born in the land of the crusty breads. Yet a recent diagnosis of diabetes in a close relative hit home and made me think again.

The Paleo Diet cuts those two culprits out—no refined sugar, no grains. Instead, meat and fish in small quantities, no or limited dairy (my homeopathic MD recently said dryly, "Dairy is overrated and usually adulterated," unless you go raw), lots of vegetables (and preferably not the starchy kind—keep it green), some fruits, as well as nuts and fats. Stories abound of healing diabetes, Celiac, and various inflammatory and auto-immune conditions by going gluten-free or following the Paleo Diet. I'm trying it.

Bloodworms and brine shrimp   August 11, 2015

My daughter loves all animals in general, and her cats in particular, to pieces. She was never afraid of animals, not even when she was little and was bitten by a big dog. A few months ago she got a Betta fish. Now she is doing extensive research on a proper diet for this predator of a fish that oftentimes only gets fed pellets and flakes in captivity. This diet can eventually lead to illness, as can feeding kibbles to cats and dogs, grain to cattle, and the Western diet to mankind. We are what we eat, and so are animals. I am so pleased that she wants to give her little fish the best possible food for his kind and realizes the importance of diet on a living thing. She told me that Betta fish thrive on bloodworms (ahem. . .), preferably live ones (not so sure about that one. . .), and brine shrimp.

This post is really not about the specifics of Betta fish food, but rather about the direct connection between diet, and health and well-being, in all living things. I wrote previously about the homemade raw food our cats thrive on, and which emulates as closely and feasibly as possible what a feline would eat in its natural habitat. The dried foods the pet food industry promotes are less than sorry versions of a carnivore's natural diet, as are packaged supermarket foods for us.

We all need our own version of bloodworms and brine shrimp.

Nose to tail September 17, 2015

Growing up, I loved eating split pea soup with smoked pig's tail. I remember seeing pigs' ears on display in our butcher shop, and we regularly ate liver and kidney. I also liked sliced beef tongue on a sandwich. Later on, when we lived in France, I had sweetbreads and brains (both very delicate and creamy-tasting), in China duck tongues (a bit tough) and chicken feet (didn't like those at all), and I still love eating headcheese on buttered German black bread with sliced pickle on top.

When we eat lobster, I collect everyone's discarded lobster heads and enjoy the innards (and that creamy green stuff) with a big glob of homemade mayonnaise at least as much as the tail and claws. Indigenous people consume every part of an animal; nothing goes to waste. In foodie countries, like France and China, every part of an animal is turned into a signature dish (*ris de veau aux morilles*—doesn't that sound delicious?). In this country, and with increasing affluence, we have turned our noses up at organ meats, and somehow have come to think of them as yucky.

In reaction the nose-to-tail movement has sprung up, and with it the art of butchering is being resurrected. In contrast to supermarket butchers, who are not trained to take a whole animal carcass apart and seldom see its innards, many young butchers are interested again in learning this craft with attention to all parts of the animal, and what to make with them (not only sausage). Organ meat (only from grass-fed animals!) is densely packed with nutrients. As a matter of fact, predators go first for the organs of a fresh kill. My acupuncturist, who is versed in Chinese nutritional principles, always reminds me to make bone broth in the wintertime and eat organ meats.

Super superfoods   February 5, 2016

A lot has been written in the past two decades on the need to return to *real food*, one-ingredient foods from Nature put together in a meal (i.e., fresh spinach sautéed with garlic and olive oil), as opposed to manufactured foods that come in boxes and packages (i.e., breakfast cereal or Western omelet mix). But evolution is always about shifts and new developments in order to evolve to higher levels. Going "back" to grandmother's foods is a good thing but not necessarily sufficient and the end-all. Our soils, even organic soils, have been depleted of minerals and trace elements, resulting in less-nourishing produce, and our bodies are subject to more pollution than ever.

Superfoods to the rescue. These are foods that are now available to us only outside their geographic growing areas, both because enlightened interest and scientific research have brought them into our awareness, and because modern transportation logistics make them accessible. Superfoods are foods with an incredible amount and array of nutritional components. Superfood guru David Wolfe has been researching superfoods for over twenty years and has written many books on various nutritional subjects. I hadn't even heard of some of his superfoods such as maca, AFA blue-green algae, or marine phytoplankton. The others on his list of ten were more familiar to me— goji berries, cacao, all bee products, spirulina, aloe vera, hempseed, and coconut. From radiation protection to cleansing the body from toxins and metals, to immune system rebuilding and activating your body's own healing powers, these new and not-so-new foods are exciting to learn about and incorporate into your meals.

It's all about the pleasure   May 11, 2016

Guilty pleasure is an uncomfortable term and particular to this country. I didn't grow up with the notion of "guilty pleasure." But here many people feel guilty about indulging because it is perceived as unvirtuous. This kind of belief might go back to this country's Puritan roots and makes for a twisted relationship with food. The result is that many feel guilty about fat (bad, bad butter; bad, bad whipped cream), about dessert and chocolate. From it came the further belief that what we enjoy tastes good but must be forbidden and bad, and what's good and healthy must taste bad (or else it couldn't possibly be good for you).

Hence the *French Paradox*. For the longest time Americans couldn't understand that French people eat fat (butter, triple *crème brie*, and *crème fraîche*), but are not necessarily fat. Of course it's not about excess and gluttony but about quality over quantity (a great little read on the subject is Mireille Guiliano's *French Women Don't Get Fat*). Maybe the recent revelations that we actually need fat in our diet, and that chocolate releases endorphins, will help to turn the tables for our enjoyment.

All that pseudo-virtuousness is not healthy for the mind. In a recent *New York Times* interview, famed French chef Eric Ripert said about food and eating, "I do not understand the idea of guilty pleasure. It's *all* about pleasure." Live a little—it's better for your mind, it's better for your body.

Eating a rainbow   August 5, 2016

Food is a multi-sensory experience of sight, smell, taste, and sensation. In continuation of the musings on the pleasure of food texture, here are some thoughts on the pleasures of color on your plate.

There is a name for the absence of color in your diet—the beige diet. Many kids are on it, but some not so adventurous adults as well. It's a diet of meat (browns) and starches (beiges—pasta, potatoes, bread), barren of fruits and vegetables, that is monochromatic and boring to look at.

I love seeing vibrant colors on my plate. The jewel tones of ripe red peppers and tomatoes, of red cabbage and eggplants' dark purple, the deep orange of bell peppers, carrots, or persimmons, summer squash's intense yellow, beets' dark garnet red, in addition to the myriad greens of broccoli, zucchini, and all the leafies are just so joyful to look at. They add to the complexity of our eating experience. In addition produce's color is an all important indicator of its varied nutritional components, besides adding visual pleasure and vibrancy to our food experience. So, do "eat a rainbow," as they say.

What's it worth it to you?   September 20, 2016

One of the main issues in the organics versus conventional food conversation is that it's not cheap. But consider that Americans spend less than ten percent of their income on food (outside and at home combined), down from about eighteen percent in 1960. Moreover, Americans spend on average less on food than eighty-three other countries worldwide.

You wouldn't argue that a simple plastic or canvas handbag costs a lot less than a well-made leather bag. It goes without saying that the leather bag will last for many years while the canvas or plastic bag will tear and deteriorate much faster. Quality materials and craftsmanship cost more because we obviously value them higher. Translate that into food and who would argue that food grown on a small farm without toxic pesticides and chemical fertilizer should cost more? It is natural that an artisanal cheese made in small batches on a small farm costs a lot more per pound than a factory made cheddar cheese made on an assembly line in huge quantities.

How you spend your money is a question of values and priorities. To me nothing is more important than what I put into my body. My life depends on it.

Making food your ally   February 10, 2017

So many people view food as their enemy. Whether it's the perception that fat is bad, that cholesterol clogs your arteries, that dessert is sinful, that foods that are good for you taste bad, or that all the yummy foods are bad for you. Well, here is a list of complaints that makes food your enemy. There is a lot of bad science behind these blanket statements, and many of them have been debunked in recent years, although it is a fact that the so-called Western diet makes us sick. It is true that eating empty calories, foods without nutritional value, will never satisfy your body, and you'll keep craving and eating more in a vicious cycle.

How about making food your ally in building a strong and energetic body instead?

When you learn to cook well with the foods that are healing and beneficial you'll make food your ally. When you learn to love good food unconditionally because it is what heals your body and assures a good life you'll make food your friend. When you become knowledgeable about the healing properties of food, the guiltless pleasures of food, you'll not only create a great hobby, but also the basis for healing the Western civilization diseases. When you learn about the good-for-you foods, and how to prepare them well so they taste delicious, you can have your cake and eat it, too.

On losing weight   April 28, 2017

Different lifestyles call for different diets. Let's face it, the majority of us have sedentary jobs. Most of us don't farm all day long, don't lift heavy equipment all day long, and are not high performance athletes. Most of the time most of us sit behind the computer much of the day, and sometimes behind the wheel or on public transportation.

Yet, our diet, in general, is still carb heavy.

Indeed, you need lots of carbs to sustain you if you have a very physical job—the way our ancestors did when they created the agricultural diet of grains and starches we still hang on to. But if you sit most of the day you don't need all that bready, noodly, ricey, potatoey type of food (sugar is a whole other bad matter—empty calories and inflammatory). Hence it's easy to gain weight on this diet.

So, if you want to lose weight, and if you don't work in construction or farming, consider cutting out some of those refined carbs and starches, and making friends with all those low-cal/low-carb vegetables such as peppers, cauliflower, broccoli, greens, asparagus, squash, mushrooms, cucumbers, eggplant, and tomatoes (I probably forgot some). Of course you'll need to make them delicious—I don't care for steamed broccoli one bit! Spice them up (the Indians have developed delicious spice combinations), combine them, sprinkle parmesan over them, broil them with olive oil until they are a bit toasty burnt on top, add lots of garlic, or butter, or sesame oil, sauce them up, puree them—*mm!*

Winging dinner   May 30, 2017

Most of the time I wing dinner. In food cultures, like China or France, many people still go shopping either every day or every few days. I don't. It's not practical for me, nor is it for most people I know. I buy my produce in bulk every other week. Meat or fish

I have in the freezer and pull out ahead of time, sometimes with a recipe in mind, most of the time not.

Whether I get produce from the co-op (once a month) or from elsewhere, I look for what looks good and is reasonably priced. That means that I usually don't shop with a produce shopping list and specific recipes in mind. It also means that I often need to invent dinner on the spot.

Usually I stick my head into the refrigerator sometime late in the afternoon, see what needs to be used as a matter of priority (greens and eggplant go first, cauliflower and peppers keep longer), what makes sense to prepare together, and whether to pair it with some meat or fish (which I will have had to thaw ahead of time—yes, I can plan that much ahead), perhaps eggs, cheese, or legumes for protein, or even some leftovers.

Sometimes I'll access my own recipe repertoire in the back of my mind, sometimes I'll look through a cookbook, often I punch a few ingredients in my phone and see what recipe comes up. A few days ago I found a terrific quinoa and fennel salad that way. Many times my dinner process is an adventure. When my daughter asks in the afternoon, "Mom, what's for dinner?" my answer is often, "We'll see," because I really won't know until I make it.

My Black Dirt dinner   June 2, 2017

"Take off your shoes." She nudged me, and I did. "Have you ever walked on Black Dirt?" she wanted to know. How lucky am I to get to feel the soft and slightly moist, gorgeously rich black dirt under my bare feet on this fabulously beautiful early summer morning, and pick my dinner?

Ahead of regular market hours, the farm sent an email inviting their regulars to come and pick the first greens of the season directly in the field. They said, "any time after nine." I jumped at the opportunity. Sure, I get my share of greens from my co-op and various other places during the cold months (produce that comes from the other side of the country). But local greens, freshly picked on the farm (by me on top of it)—are so much better. Rhubarb, baby turnips (the greens are the healthiest part!), broccoli rabe, spinach, and Persian cucumbers from the greenhouse are my loot from this morning.

If you're an avid gardener, you may smile at my excitement as you walk out your door and into your vegetable garden to pick your dinner. As a transplanted city girl, with an herb patch and a few eggplant and kale plants for good measure, I am excited. The remembrance of this morning's Black Dirt expedition will live in tonight's dinner. Deep food—it's all about the experience.

No size fits all   July 18, 2017

You are unique, your digestive system is unique, your food preferences are unique, your constitution, in combination with ethnic provenance and health history, is unique.

It's okay to critically read books on diet trends (paleo, ketogenic, vegan, vegetarian, flexitarian, ethnic, what have you), or on nutrition, in order to become informed on the state of our food and its profound influence on our well-being. But then you need to test these theories mindfully on your own body to understand what agrees with you and what doesn't, what aggravates certain conditions or alleviates them, what gives you energy, what regulates your weight, what helps you heal. The one exception I'll make is refined sugar. It's not good for anybody. Period.

We like to simplify and standardize, but imagine what would happen if some diet fundamentalist prescribed the same diet for all seven billion people on this planet?

Digestive systems have adapted over hundreds and thousands of years to what is available geographically. Prescribe a vegetarian diet to an Inuit, or an Inuit diet to a Hindu—okay, these are extreme analogies—and they would likely become ill. So take all you read, all that people say, with a grain of salt—then see what *really*

applies to your own condition and constitution. Although I have already cut out a lot of grain from my diet (and lost quite a bit of weight in the process), I am currently trying this gluten-free thing. I'm really not convinced this is necessary for me—we'll see, hoping to prove myself wrong.

No diet applies to all—which one is the right one for you?

Rebooting your system

Sometimes your system needs a reboot. Mine does, and I am doing a one-day liquid fast as I write this. Did you know that sixty percent of your daily energy consumption goes towards running your digestive system and the digestion of solid foods? That only leaves forty percent for everything else—work, play, and healing. If you can free that sixty percent for a short period of time by refraining from solid foods for a day or two, it can do wonders for cleansing and healing your body. Drinking lots of liquids during that time—vegetable juices, green juices, fruit juices (always in moderation because of the high sugar content), broth, lemon water with a bit of maple syrup, some tea, lots of water—literally reboots your system, cleans you out, gives your digestive tract a break, and frees up that energy for healing your body.

It's interesting to note that many religions include fasting in one form or another in their rituals. Some people are religious about regular fasts (pun intended), such as a liquid day a month; some people fast for two or three days whenever they feel their system needs it. Fasting is a time-honored practice that makes a lot of sense, although it's not indicated for everyone (so make sure you consult your health care practitioner for advice if you've never done this and have doubts or questions).

Why not give it a try? It will leave you energized.

On
sustainability

Free clothes drier   May 21, 2012

When energy prices spiked several years back I remembered
the European clothes- drying racks of my childhood that are still
customary over there (neither my parents in Germany, nor my sister in Belgium, have driers). I ordered two racks over the internet
and have dried our clothes for free ever since. My electric clothes
drier gets used only very rarely anymore. These racks are inexpensive, and you can find them on this side of the Atlantic as well.

In comparison to the stationary racks sometimes found in gardens or the overhead clothes lines strung between trees, I can
move my racks outside when the weather is nice, and inside during
the cold months. Moreover, when there are no clothes to be dried,
I don't have to look at the rack in the garden. They fold up flat
and store behind a door or against a wall. Between my two racks,
I can fit three loads of laundry, and when the air is dry the laundry
dries in a few hours.

Why do you want to do that?   February 26, 2013

That is what we've heard many times since beginning the planning process for our new energy-efficient house. The most extensive argument may well have been around the merits of triple-pane
windows. In northern Europe triple-pane windows are now standard for new construction, and Canadians already use them exten-
sively. But here in the U.S., energy awareness is still in its infancy,
and we kept being asked, "What do you want to do that for?"

In comparing windows, we found that Canadians build better
frames, which makes a big difference, and they use orientation and
climate-specific glazing for optimal energy savings. European
casement windows have a much tighter fit than the double-hung
windows typical for here because of the different frame design.
Passive House windows are the platinum standard: It tops them

all (price included!).

Thinking ahead, Germans are already talking about quadruple windows!

Stuff, stuff, and more stuff   April 12, 2013

Have you ever given trash, yours or that of others, much thought? Here are some statistics. The average amount of waste each person generates in a day increased from 2.68 pounds in 1960 to 4.5 pounds in 1990. Luckily, that number has held steady due to recycling efforts. But it still totals about 1.35 billion pounds a day nationwide, or 251 million tons a year! And this only accounts for *personal* trash, which constitutes two percent of the waste stream—yikes for the industrial waste stream! But let's stay with our personal garbage, because that's where we can make a difference.

The first rule of thumb is that recycling and composting are good, but buying less stuff is better. Besides, it's been documented that we can't gain happiness through consumption. Elizabeth Royte, who wrote the very enlightening book *Garbageland*, says, "We don't need better ways to get rid of things. We need to *not* get rid of things, either by keeping them cycling through the system or not. . .desiring them in the first place."

But once we have garbage, what are our choices? They are: dumping, incinerating, and recycling. FYI—in untreated landfills, waste can take forty to fifty years to decompose, in treated landfills between five and ten. Yet plastics may take hundreds of years to decompose! And there are other problems with landfills—their toxicity (supposedly landfills are the largest source of human-generated greenhouse gases, although CAFOs, those enormous industrial animal-feeding operations that make supermarket meat, are also huge culprits), and the ever-increasing amounts of garbage and landfill space needed (a) because of population increase, and

(b) because our consumer society model is based on ever-increasing consumption—the system breaks down if we stop consuming, and then the politicians scream "recession": Stop screaming with them).

So, what can you do?

Don't pick up any more plastic bags from the supermarket, bring your own cloth bags. Consume less, recycle and compost more. Use compostable garbage bags, recycled paper products, and products made from recycled plastic. Buy more groceries and cleaning supplies in bulk, reuse your glass jars and Chinese takeout plastic containers (I wish they would take them back, since I don't like plastic in the first place), reuse your Ziploc bags a few times. Subscribe to Freecycle (it's all about giving and getting for free). Donate your gently used unwanted stuff instead of throwing it away. Buy clothes at second-hand stores (I am a huge fan). Most of all - stop wanting, wanting, wanting stuff.

Where your values are   August 6, 2013

In the spring we switched our electric energy supplier to Viridian and chose one- hundred-percent renewable energy (they also have a twenty-percent renewable energy option). Viridian is a socially responsible (another worthwhile value) power company that supplies clean energy from local wind power. I found that cheaper is not necessarily better, because cheaper is no longer my only value and consideration when making a purchase. Oh, I do admit that I buy things at Walmart—where else can I get sewing thread, school notebooks, cotton socks, a sink stopper, pens and envelopes, and marshmallows for our camping trip, all in one place? And at Trader Joe's (lots of inexpensive organics). But then they have certain values attached to them, which I buy into. Walmart (the new Woolworth) offers lots of different utilitarian things in one place (important, since I live in the country and have few specialty stores), and Trader Joe's means organics for the masses.

I am conscientious about what I buy and where I buy it—meat from local farmers (or venison from our own fall harvest); produce from the food co-op, local farm stands, or the farmers market; organic grocery staples in bulk from the co-op; eggs from a friend or a local farmer; clothes for myself and my daughter mostly from local second-hand stores; pet supplies from the local pet store for the corn-based cat litter (and I make my own cat food), one-hundred-percent recycled copy paper for the office from Staples (only place that has it); and one-hundred-percent recycled toilet paper and paper towels from Trader Joe's (lots less than the local supermarket), to name just a few choices that indicate clear values.

Imagine what would happen if eighty percent of Americans stopped buying genetically modified corn and soy products? And remember, if you don't buy organic they'll keep spraying the pesticides that are killing the bees, which are our main produce pollinators!

Be aware of what values you fund, or *don't* fund, with your purchases. Cheap is not the only value.

On sustainability   September 27, 2013

You may wonder what all the sustainability and "green" practices buzz is about, and what it actually means. Most of our current manufacturing processes are linear, energy intense, and create waste, thus damaging the environment one way or the other.

Just imagine how corn flakes are made (not that I'm an expert). The various ingredients—genetically modified corn, food coloring, high-fructose corn syrup, preservatives, and additives—have to be shipped to the corn flakes factory from various locations by way of a lot of energy (trucking, gas) and packaging material. The packaging waste of the corn flakes ingredients goes into the garbage or recycling stream (if we are lucky). Then the cereal is manufactured by machines, with high-energy input and some waste products (water, steam, and fumes, and who knows what else). After that the corn flakes get packaged into sealed inner plastic bags and outer cardboard boxes (another high-energy–high-supply input process), and shipped to distributors (trucking, gas—you get the picture), then to the supermarkets, where they have to recycle or throw away the pallets, shrink wrap, and outer cartons. Finally, the cereal gets purchased, and the retail packaging goes into the waste (the inside plastic pouch) or gets recycled (the exterior cardboard box). Overall it's a process that requires huge material and energy inputs all along, and creates enormous waste and pollution.

A sustainable process should require no exterior input of energy or material. It is a cyclical and wasteless process that repeats itself indefinitely without damage or side effects to the environment. The easiest example of such a process is a vegetable garden. If we save the seeds from one year to the next, if we fertilize with compost created from organic home and garden waste, if we use manual labor to tend to it, it becomes a wasteless, indefinitely renewable cycle that requires no outside energy or product purchase other than elbow grease. All natural cycles are thus sustainable. Permaculture is also such a sustainable agricultural/cultural system.

On the home front, the better our houses are insulated for example, the less outside energy we need to introduce to heat and cool them, and the more sustainable the home energy cycle becomes. The Passive House is a residential building concept with such stringent insulation specifications that the house retains a constant temperature and requires no heating system (heating the hot water is another story, and energy to run appliances and lighting is yet another). A Passive House takes into account the heat output from lights, people, and appliances in its energy calculations. Then there is a zero-energy house, which is sustainable and generates its own energy needs. A zero-energy house may include a geothermal heating/cooling system, solar panels to offset the electrical needs, LED lighting (the light bulbs are good for fifty thousand hours! - something like twenty years, and consume minimal energy), triple-pane windows, and a few other new cutting edge mechanical systems, in addition to superior insulation.

Sustainable is the way to go, it is gentle on the planet!

It's happening   January 24, 2014

In a way I'm an intuitive trend tracker, and I think it's happening. The *New York Times* declared on its front page today, "Industry Awakens to Threat of Climate Change."

Climate change is real and happening faster than we anticipated; it will have huge impacts worldwide on all fronts, and for each of us personally (and more so for our children). The faster we jointly act on reversing the causes, the less painful the effects will be in the long run (although all that carbon we are spewing into the atmosphere will stay around for at least a thousand years, even if we reverse its continuous increase now).

Waking up and acting is what's required *now*. And while we, as individuals, can make a big difference by opting for renewable electric energy sources, switching to LED lamps, putting solar panels on our houses, and insulating our homes, opting for double- and triple-pane windows, buying and working local—just to name a few efforts that have impact if practiced by lots of people (the effect is cumulative)—the real difference is when this thinking finally bleeds into the commercial-industrial sector. And that's what's happening—finally. It is encouraging, even though the commercial-industrial sector is partially coming from the perspective of the bottom line instead of the ecoperspective.

But it's a start.

Bring your own bags   February 28, 2014

I have never liked the ubiquitous plastic shopping bags the supermarkets and other big box stores almost force on you. They fly around parking lots on a windy day and end up in shrubs and trees as well as in our oceans (have you heard of the Pacific trash vortex?). And even though I save those few I inevitably end up with, in my kitchen cabinet with the other recyclables, I mostly have no use for them.

People have certainly become more aware in recent years, what with all those bags made from recycled plastic bottles you can get at every supermarket (although they don't wash well). In Europe it has always been customary to bring your own shopping bag, net, or basket. In more recent times plastic shopping bags, at least in Germany, have become so expensive to buy (they don't hand them out for free over there) that it has drastically curtailed their use. California may soon become the first state in this country to ban this environmental scourge.

I use machine-washable canvas shopping bags, of which I bought a whole bunch many years ago, as well as a really neat bottle-carrying bag (it fits nine bottles). I usually have a few in my car, just in case. Traditional woven shopping baskets are no longer very practical because they are bulky and you can't fit a lot into them. Mesh shopping bags, on the other hand, fold up so small you can always carry one in your bag for unforeseen purchases.

We begin to become environmentally aware in baby steps. This is one way to start.

Lightbulb 101   March 4, 2014

As the traditional pear-shaped, incandescent light bulbs are being phased out altogether (2009 in Europe, 2014 in this country), LED lights are pushing in and will eventually eclipse even fluorescents, compact and otherwise.

Just from a lifespan perspective, the difference is staggering. Conventional incandescents last about twelve hundred hours (about half a year at an average conservative use of six hours per day), halogens two thousand, compact fluorescents about eight thousand hours (about three and a half years), linear fluorescents about twenty thousand hours (about nine years), while LED light bulbs last a whopping fifty thousand hours (that's twenty-three years).

LED light bulbs cost a lot more, at least right now. But that's an initial investment that pays in the long run, and drastically reduces your electric bill and maintenance costs. LEDs use only about one tenth of the electricity of the old light bulbs, and half that of a compact fluorescent. So the light output of a fifty-watt incandescent bulb can be replicated with an eight-watt LED, and they are less toxic for the environment.

That's what an investment is—an upfront expense for later gain. When we buy organic food, or pastured meat, we make an investment into the health of our body via the higher upfront cost of the healthier food. Same with LED light bulbs, we make an investment into a lower electric bill and a reduced light bulb replacement cost (and ultimately a reduction of fossil fuel consumption).

Imagine not having to change a light bulb for another two decades?

How big is your garbage can?   March 28, 2014

Actually, I should ask, "How big is your recycling can?" I am hoping that your recycling can is bigger than your garbage can. If so, you are on the right track. If not, there is a lot you can do to reverse that.

At our house we have the smallest garbage can available, a thirty-five gallon can, while our recycling can is huge, it takes ninety-five gallons. I am a fervent recycler, as well as bottle (to the store to get my five cents back) and egg carton (I get my eggs from a farm) and plastic bag returner (to the supermarket collection bin for all sorts of plastic bags I somehow end up with). We usually generate only about one full garbage bag made of recyclable plastic per week (sometimes two) for our family of four (and about half of that is produce and other compostable stuff). Everything else gets recycled.

Moreover, where we live, recycling services are cost-free (or rather paid through our taxes), while we pay for our garbage pickup by can size—the smaller our garbage can, the less we pay. And if you have a garden and can compost, you'll end up with even less garbage.

So you can do something good for the environment and save money on top of that (although this goes beyond the mere money question, since we pay a huge environmental price for every bit of irresponsibility).

Eat less meat! April 16, 2014

How preposterous of me to tell you so? No. Surprisingly, this is a huge environmental issue that goes way beyond the potentially ethical question of killing (they call it "harvesting" now, to make it sound more harmless) a living being and eating it. I'm not a vegetarian. However, in the Western industrialized world meat consumption has skyrocketed from eating meat once a week or so to just under two hundred pounds per person per year in the U.S. since the advent of cheap meat. This enormous meat consumption, in combination with the rise in world population and the increasing number of people able to afford the cheap meat, has become a recipe for disaster.

The environmental calamity arises both from "cheap" and "too much." Why? Because the CAFOs (concentrated animal feeding operations) that these poor animals are raised in are among the biggest greenhouse gas emitters on this planet—generating about eighteen percent of greenhouse gases. In addition, the huge amounts of animal waste leach antibiotics into our ground water. And to top it off, the conditions under which these sorry souls are being raised, then killed and processed are so horrendous as to be literally unbelievable (read Jonathan Safran Foer because you must know).

Depending on many factors there is nothing necessarily wrong with eating meat *per se*. As a matter of fact, especially during childhood and adolescence, animal protein helps to grow the brain. But, like with anything, balance is the key and industrialized nations have become meat addicted. Food researcher and author Marion Nestlé has advocated eating meat in condiment quantities.

How can we help? First and foremost by resisting buying cheap supermarket meat, which comes from CAFOs. Instead, buy your meat at or from a local farm where the animals have been raised sustainably. Yes, it will cost more. But we ought to consume much less of it! That's the point. It's in the quality, not the quantity.

Climate marching   September 23, 2014

Our family climate marched this past Sunday 9/21—yes, it's a verb now. And I think we must do this every year from now on, until "We The People" get the message to our politicians to act *now*, not later, because later is too late. Together with three hundred to four hundred thousand fellow protesters in New York City, and tens of thousands more in all corners of the world, from Paris to Melbourne, from Berlin to London and Rio, we participated in what MIT researcher Jesse Jenkins called "one of America's largest mass protests," and Amy Davidson of the *New Yorker* described as "the largest climate change protest in history."

It was powerful and emotional to experience so much synergy and togetherness on the single most important issue of our times, which, if we are successful in shifting, will propel us beyond the singularly profit-oriented oil age into a more co-creative and aware age of Earth stewardship.

From the perspective of our evolving human consciousness this is the first time in history that we are awakening to the incredible realization, empowering but also sobering, that we can actually change and steer our existence, that our consciousness and drive are what creates everything around us. We don't all have to become activists. But we all can do our bit to help this momentous evolutionary process along, whether by buying more organics, insulating our homes, getting a more fuel efficient car, eating less meat (and preferably only the sustainably raised kind), buying less stuff and recycling more, and voting environmentally aware politicians into office.

I'd love to hear what you are doing to help since, as one of the signs at the march said, "There is no Planet B."

Less (paper) waste   *January 6, 2015*

Since we take (too many) trees down to make paper, it makes sense to become more aware of the amount of paper we use and be diligent about it. Let's try to reduce its use, save it, reuse it, or at least recycle it. Paper can be recycled multiple times before it becomes unfit for another cycle.

Reading your paper online, your books on an e-device, and sending emails and e-cards (and who writes paper thank-you-cards anymore?) helps to reduce the amount of paper that needs to be manufactured. Although tedious, unsubscribing from catalogs you don't want is an important action. I save and reuse paper gift bags if they are in good condition. And in general, I am a dedicated, bordering on obsessive, recycler of all household paper and cardboard, such as cereal and other cardboard packaging, newspapers and magazines, Amazon shipping boxes (if I can't reuse them for sending out something else), envelopes, toilet paper and paper towel rolls (if I find them in the garbage I will take them out).

Since I get me eggs from friends or local farms I always bring the egg cartons back for reuse. Books you no longer want can be donated to your local library, or be given to friends who have not read them.

In my home office I make double-sided copies and print on back pages (the kids generate tons of one-sided school related paper I print on). I also use shredded paper as packing material instead of the terribly environmentally unfriendly packing peanuts, or bubble wrap (I shred everything with a name and address on it, which makes for quite a bit of packing material).

If you do need to buy paper and paper goods—and we can't get around basics such as toilet paper and paper towels, paper napkins for the occasional party, or copy paper—consider buying products made from one hundred percent recycled paper. But even I have my limits—I don't buy tissues made from recycled paper because I find them scratchy.

Less (household) waste   January 13, 2015

And now for the last installment on reducing waste. It is better for the environment and our landfills if we keep as much waste out of them as possible.

The first tip to reducing household waste is to buy less stuff (especially stuff of the plastic kind), and to buy more carefully. We live a life of luxury and abundance (even if it doesn't always seem that way), are tempted by the many bargains and sales that pressure us into buying, and often make spontaneous purchases that we don't need or even like (hence buyer's remorse). With regard to the quality over quantity argument, my dad used to say that he "can't afford to buy cheap." What he meant was that cheap stuff breaks faster and therefore needs to be replaced faster, so ultimately costs more (and creates more waste). Better to buy good quality items, even if they are more expensive upfront. They will last longer and are a better investment in the long run.

Next tip is to recycle and buy recycled, aka second hand. This also reduces the amount of things that need to be manufactured, and the amount of things going into the waste stream. I buy a lot of clothes at second hand shops (I find more interesting things there, and I dislike mall shopping with passion), donate unwanted furnishing items to a local shelter coordinator, and unwanted books to my local library. You can also resell your books on cash4books.net, as a friend recently pointed out. There are second hand shops for furniture now, and then there are whole organizations, such as Freecycle.org, that do nothing but help people shuffle their unwanted stuff around. Check it out, they have local chapters everywhere.

And lastly, I use www.ourcommonplace. com/your location quite frequently for either donating and selling items, or requesting things I need. A while ago I needed reusable name tag holders for a local non-profit, and found them for free from someone who had a box of them stashed away that they no longer needed. More recently, we were looking for a ping pong table, and I asked the local Commonplace forum whether anyone was selling one. Lo and behold, a kind neighbor offered us one for free.

Trash free   February 20, 2015

San Francisco diverts eighty percent of its trash from landfills. Its goal is to become a zero-waste city by 2020, meaning that no household garbage goes back into the waste stream, but instead will be entirely recycled or composted (industrial and commercial garbage is a much greater challenge yet).

We recycle everything we possibly can. Besides the obvious, such as newspapers and glass jars, it includes toilet paper and paper towel rolls, yogurt cups, aluminum foil, all recyclable plastic bagging or packaging, gift wrap, paper tags and what not. In an average week (meaning no parties) our family of four produces about one big thirteen-gallon (biodegradable) garbage bag full of waste. That includes what ought to go onto the compost pile (tea leaves, produce scraps, egg shells, coffee grounds, tissues and paper towels). Once we compost again our waste output should be about half a big trash bag full per week.

Windy power   December 22, 2015

While solar has been all the rage for a few years now, wind power is following close behind. The Paris Climate Summit was a clear success, even though it comes a bit late in the game. Now we have to hustle. We are putting more solar panels on our house in the spring so we can be net-zero and so our solar energy production meets our entire energy consumption—our current array only covers forty-five percent.

Scientific American announced yesterday that the highly appealing thirty percent tax credit for solar and wind installations (on parts and labor!), that was supposed to run out at the end of 2016, has been extended through the end of the decade for now. This is a huge incentive in combination with state tax credits and NYSERDA credits (for those who live in New York—each state has different incentives).

Wind power will now be following in solar's footsteps for homes, small businesses, and farms. The *Times* just reported that small rooftop wind turbines are being installed along the same model as residential rooftop solar panels, many of them in leased deals.

Go for it, whether solar or wind!

Library of things   *January 8, 2016*

Perhaps a better way to understand the new sharing economy than using Uber or
Airbnb's services (after all these businesses are for-profit) is through a "library of things." I really like the idea. A similar principle already exists in the form of seed banks, from which you can obtain seeds as long as you bring back seeds from your harvest at the end of the season to replenish the seed bank.

Libraries of Things go beyond lending books, movies, and magazines. They lend tools, equipment, or things to community members. The benefits are multifold. For one, you as an individual won't need to invest in the cost of, say, an expensive 3-D printer to experiment with it, or buy a pair of snowshoes for that once-in-a-while winter hike. The investment happens at the community level, for which we all chip in via our local taxes.

At the same time an economy in manufacturing develops because less stuff needs to be made. Moreover, access to such a library reduces the stuff you need to store and upkeep. It is likely that you only use your hedge clippers or power drill a few times a year. Why not borrow one from a tool library instead of buying a brand new, expensive tool that sits idle most of the time, collects dust, and takes up real estate in your garage? Along similar lines there are hour exchanges, where you swap other people's time, help, and experience for services you need, against your own time.

All these are neat sharing ideas to explore, and present opportunities to meet new people.

Going sustainably   *February 26, 2016*

We tend to bury our burial wishes, because we don't really want to think about death and dying. My husband and I decided quite a while ago to be cremated and our ashes thrown into the wind—from whence we came. Perhaps it's a bit more sustainable than embalming the body in all kinds of chemicals for an open-cask viewing (which I personally find kind of creepy), spending all kinds of money on a casket that takes twenty-five years to decompose, and both body and casket leeching all kinds of yucky chemicals into the soil (and our ground water). But even the burning is a toxic and energy-intensive process.

Did you know that embalmers have to wear "full body armor" while embalming, because of the toxic fumes associated with the preservation chemicals? There are more sustainable burial practices than cremation, from the weird (we saw the Jain funeral towers in Bombay from afar many years ago, where the bodies are laid out in the open on top of the towers and the vultures take care of them) to the simple (wrapping the body in a shroud and burying it without casket and chemicals).

Better yet may be this method: One of my faithful blog readers (thank you, Alice) reminded me of this 2011 TED Talk by MIT-trained artist Jae Rhim Lee. Lee has created a mycological burial suit embedded with mushroom capsules that assist in the quick decomposition of the body and digestion of toxins. The suit incorporates mushroom spores that allow mushrooms to grow and use the body as feeding ground while composting it all completely and sustainably. Cheap and non-toxic! Watch the talk on her website Coeio.

I think I'll change my mind about cremation, now that I know about the mushroom burial suit.

Super crop   March 1, 2016

You can eat it in seed, flour, or oil form, you can make clothes and rope from it, as well as biodiesel fuel, paper, and building materials. Meet hemp, the old/new super crop. Pretty much the only thing you can't do with hemp is get high on it, because it's not the same as marijuana, although they both belong to the cannabis family. It's a super plant and super food that withstands drought, thrives in poor soil, and grows fast.

Hemp oil is extremely rich in essential fatty acids, and according to David Wolfe of Superfood fame, ". . .the only known food with ideal ratios of omega-6 and omega-3 fatty acids." The oil is also used in body care products. Hempseed is a complete protein, the leaves are edible, and you can make tea with them. The seeds can be made into butter, bread, beer, and milk similar to nut milk. Hemp's fiber is one of the strongest fibers on Earth, hence its use for rope. But it can also be made into clothing. Hemp clothing is better than cotton in every way—warmer, more absorbent, stronger and more resilient, accepts dye better, extremely durable, and it becomes softer and more comfortable the longer you wear it.

Hemp can grow pretty much anywhere in the world and yields two and a half times the fiber the same area planted with cotton would yield. A biodegradable plastic can be made from the stalk, as well as building materials like insulation, fiberboard, and hempcrete, all non-toxic and non off-gassing.

Hopefully, the silly hemp ban in the U.S., that dates back to the 1930s and was engineered around political and monetary interests, will be lifted soon as people become more aware of this super crop.

A million years! April 16, 2016

I am a bit obsessive-compulsive when it comes to recycling because I want to make sure nothing that doesn't need to go to the landfill goes there. In the kitchen, in the spot originally designed for the trashcan, I have a big recycling bin for the usual paper/glass jars/bottles/various packaging items, which the weekly collection truck picks up. A canvas bag hangs behind the pantry door for the redeemable bottles and cans, for which I get back 5 cents each from the supermarket. In another canvas bag behind the pantry door I collect recyclable plastic bags—the supermarket has a drop-off bin for them. And then I have a bucket for all the produce scraps, eggshells, and tea leaves that we compost in the composting bin in the backyard. I recycle clothing six ways from Sunday—by giving it away, bringing it to the second hand or thrift shops in my area, or dropping it into one of the many clothing drops. Cable, phone stuff, and very small electronics go to Best Buy, but a few old phones are lingering on the hallway table while I am trying to figure out what to do with them.

My son always comments that the back of my car looks like a junkyard. Indeed, it can get crowded back there, between the mountain of reusable shopping bags, two freezer bags (you never know), various items waiting to be dropped off somewhere, and the carton I use to safely transport my weekly raw milk, yogurt, and egg order back from the farm.

The only thing I am really frustrated about is Styrofoam. They don't accept it for recycling anywhere in our area, and it will linger in the landfill for a million or so years.

Small is beautiful   May 25, 2016

Ice cream servings in a cone are small in Europe, probably a bit less than half the size of the big scoops we are used to over here. Generally, we equate *big* with *good* because bigger is better, right? Cars used to be the size of boats in this country, until people became more energy aware. "How was the food at that new restaurant?" "It was great, we had a lot of food." But how did it taste? May be the portion was too large if you took half your meal home in a doggy bag.

E.F. Schumacher was way ahead in 1973, when he argued in his economic classic *Small is Beautiful* that building our economy on eternal growth is not sustainable. Indeed, our planet doesn't expand. Around the same time Frances Moore Lappé wrote *Diet for a Small Planet*. She pioneered the discussion around the terrible environmental impact our industrial "meat production" causes, and argued for vegetarianism.

Interest rates have been shrinking, they are even lower in Europe than here, and discussions on negative interest rates are popping up—getting penalized for leaving your money in the bank. We may eventually need to spend it or put it under the mattress.

These are signs that small is beautiful, that bigger is not sustainable, and that our economies need to shrink in order to halt the consumerist excess and environmental damage we have created. Think quality over quantity. "How delicious was that meal?" not "How big was it?" "What beautiful material is that dress made of?" not "Buy two for the price of one."

Keep enjoying   December 9, 2016

We have created a throw-away society to feed The Economy. We are used to so much abundance, and granted, it's often cheaper to replace something than to have it fixed. But this habit encourages needless consumption and expenses, more trash, and the making of more (cheap) stuff.

In the fall people go on mum buying sprees, and by Thanksgiving the wilted plants end up on the compost pile. But mums are perennials. They may not come back entirely as vibrantly as the first year, but they don't deserve the trash treatment, you can plant them in your garden. Same thing with poinsettias. They have become such a Christmas industry because people buy them new each year. Lo and behold, the three poinsettias I received as a gift last year are blooming for the second time around, and just in time for Christmas.

Spend less and keep enjoying.

Net-zero   June 10, 2016

We are finally net-zero after having added more solar panels on our other two roofs this spring. Our original panels met forty-five percent of our electric needs; together with the new panels we should produce enough power to meet all our electric needs—for heating and air-conditioning, hot water, lighting, household appliances, as well as home office computers and office machines. No fossil fuels—clean and silent energy.

Taking the federal and state tax credits into account, the payback on purchasing solar panels is somewhere around seven to nine years for us. Given that the panels are good for twenty to twenty-five years, we expect between eleven and sixteen years of free utilities. Not bad, considering that energy costs are steadily inching up, and fossil fuels are on their way out. At today's rates that translates very roughly into a fifty-two-to- seventy-five-thousand-dollar savings over the life of the panels

How would you like to put that kind of savings towards paying off your mortgage early or your kids' college fund?

*Spiritual
meanderings*

Taking charge June 1, 2012

A brief bout with mild depression a years ago taught me an important lesson and helped me to shift my thinking drastically. At that time I felt like a victim of circumstances, believing that the world was to blame for where I was at in life. I even went to an allopathic doctor and got myself some pills. But then something shifted in my mind. I realized that I create my life, my circumstances, my opportunities, the way I perceive everything around me, out of my own consciousness and beliefs, and that those are not static, I can change them.

I brought the unopened pills back to the pharmacy and took charge of my life. It is not only incredibly empowering to wake up to this wonderfully creative opportunity of shaping and creating my future today and every day, it is also an awesome responsibility. And it has implications for the people around us.

Martin Luther King famously said something along the lines of, "Only when you are at your best can I be at my best, and only when I am at my best, can you be at your best." The more we realize our own creative potential, the more we illuminate everything and everyone around us.

Putting on lipstick June 11, 2012

Swami Rudrananda, the spiritual teacher also known as Rudi, used to say that your spiritual practice begins with making your bed in the morning. Although I do make my bed in the morning, my day begins with putting on lipstick. What Rudi meant, though, was that your spiritual and your everyday life are one and the same, and your everyday life has to be in order as a basis for a good spiritual practice. It is misguided to neglect your everyday life for the lofty pursuit of a removed spiritual life.

One such example was published in last week's *Times* about a three-year yoga retreat that ended prematurely with a fatal consequence for one participant. The participants had removed themselves from practical life for three years. The better idea is to interweave your spiritual convictions and practice with your material life.

Since most of my work happens in front of my computer at home, I need to get myself, and the house, in order before doing anything else; part of that is dressing up nicely and putting lipstick on. After that I am ready for the day.

Same time next year   *June 22, 2012*

It is comforting to me to live in awareness of the circularity of life. That's why I have always minded my children's six-day lesson schedule for a five-day week. It goes against the grain and is confusing. Not that, "If it's Tuesday it must be meatloaf" is such an inspired idea, but there is something to be said about, "If it's Tuesday, we must have Art."

Today is my birthday, and I like the notion that it comes back year after year, like all of the holidays. In reality, though, nothing ever stays the same. Perhaps because of that, because life is all about change, the regularity of circular rhythms such as the seasons, the planetary revolutions, the tides, the full moons, the reoccurrence of our birthdays, even the rhythm of the school year, builds a reassuring structure from where to watch and live the change.

Children, who grow up with a strong awareness of these rhythms, as they teach it for example in Waldorf education, can become grounded adults. And as an adult I am learning to see the circularity of life beyond my own death as a continuous cycle—in and out of physical life, in and out of non-physical existence—in an even grander perspective.

Wordlessness September 10, 2012

I admit I did not get it for a long time, the "don't think," the "drop into your heart space," or "count from one to ten and then start over" effort to get "out of my mind." Finally I did get it when I recently read Martha Beck's new book *Finding Your Way In A Wild New World*.

She spoke about dropping into "wordlessness." That's it! Somehow I understood that analogy a lot better than all of the others, and a light bulb went off. It's as if there was a word world floating in, around, and above us that engulfs us. We name everything, categorize everything, judge everything, and clad everything into words. However, words lock our experience, our vision into our individual perspective with our particular set of emotions attached to it. On the other hand, when you drop out of that framework by leaving the words by the wayside, everything simply is the way it is—it is not tinted with the meaning of words.

When I slip out of this word cloud that surrounds me I find myself in a space where there is only feeling, seeing, sensing, being. That world is devoid of anxiety, anger, and all of the other negative emotions, because those arise only out of the connection between words, past experience, and future expectations. Try it sometime!

Life's yummy factor September 19, 2012

Holistic comes from *whole* and also *holy* and means that something includes both the qualitative and the quantitative, seen and unseen, physical and metaphysical aspects. Our culture is a bit lopsided because it has favored the quantitative aspect of science over the spiritual aspect, at least since Isaac Newton.

But the qualitative aspect, the spiritual, the unseen, is what adds the yummy factor to life. Knowledge of the calories of a strawberry, or its vitamin content, is pretty dull and meaningless without the smell of the ripe fruit, the visual appreciation of its red ripeness, the feeling of the teeth sinking into the juicy flesh, and finally that distinct sweet strawberry taste on the tongue.

The yummy factor is what makes life worth living.

The heart as portal, not pump   September 25, 2012

This past weekend my meditation teacher equated the heart with a portal to within, to infinite self-love and compassion. Rudolf Steiner said over a century ago that our human destiny would change once we recognized that the heart is not a pump. There are two interesting articles on that, one by Thomas Cowan, M.D., and the other by researchers from Temple University. Both articles refute the pump idea from the perspective of fluid dynamics and propose an alternate way of understanding the heart. Perhaps rearranging this understanding of the mechanics will lead us to recognize our interface with the spiritual.

Consider our cultural symbolism of the heart as the center of love, as an expression of our compassion. I like the portal analogy, especially after reading Harry Potter and its many portals, unassuming gateways to much larger realities, unrecognized and untapped by those not in the know.

Food for thought indeed.

Perfection of opposites   September 28, 2012

The beauty in this gray rainy day today lies in its perfection. It is not *bad* weather; rather it simply *is*, and it is perfect. While we consider it something like an opposite to a sunny day with blue skies, it helps to see it instead in a more holistic way, as the flip side of the same thing as the sunny day.

Take night and day as an example. The concept of night is entwined with the concept of day. They do not exist in isolation.

And both are continuously on their way towards each other. They are not mutually exclusive, and one is not better or worse than the other. They both simply are an aspect of each other, and therein lies the perfection.

Mirror mirror   December 14, 2012

Did you ever wonder why the world may seem full of wonder and beauty one day, and gray and miserable the next? It's the same world after all, the world hasn't changed suddenly.

We see the world through our emotions, or I could say that the world reflects back to us our state of mind. If you have never thought about it in this way, it might seem far fetched or even crazy. What, there is no objective world out there that "is the way it is?" No, everything is in the eyes of the beholder. Even quantum physics says so.

Think about it. If you have endured a calamity, or you are simply down and out, the world appears utterly bleak to you. Yet, the same world simultaneously appears full of magic to someone freshly in love. We tend to blame people, situations, or the state of affairs of our world for our experiences; we put the cause outside ourselves. In reality it works the other way round. We attract, or get mirrored, our state of mind through interaction with our environment. A shift in emotions, a shift in beliefs and values, shifts how we experience everything around us.

Looking at your experiences, your life, from this amazing perspective opens up a world of possibilities for spiritual growth.

It's all about people   January 24, 2013

Life is really all about people. We can't live in a vacuum, or on a lonely island for that matter. We feel an affinity to other people who are similar to us, and thus see reflected back to us how we are already. When we dislike something in another person, it mirrors our shadow side back to us, something we still need to learn or accept. This means that we define ourselves in comparison to and with the help of others. It's truly enlightening to look at it that way.

What's holistic, anyway?   May 13, 2013

Some people whom I have spoken to about *living holistically* think it just means eating your veggies and going to the gym, sort of just leading a pretty healthy life. But it's more than that. The word "holistic" is a cross between "whole" and "holy." Why "whole?" Or we could ask: what is not whole and needs to be put together again? Life consists of both the invisible and the visible, the spiritual and the material, soul/mind and body, thought and matter. These last few centuries we have been living as if the spiritual or invisible part of life (our emotions, beliefs, feelings, spirituality) did not exist. And we felt proud of it, proud of being "rational" and "analytical," proud of focusing on the "real" stuff we can see, touch, feel, smell, and hear, not that wishy-washy, airy-fairy emotional stuff no one can see and that's not really "real."

Turns out, though, that that stuff we tend to push under the rug is pretty important.

Without it we mistreat and rape Nature (because we think it's separate from us), we make war (because we think "they" are different from us), we don't vote (because we think it makes no difference), we treat animals worse than things (because we think they are not sentient beings), we buy as cheap as possible (because we don't think of the people behind the product, i.e. the Bangladesh clothing factory collapse)—or maybe we don't even think at all.

Holistic means putting the two sides together again, the way they belong, the way they are, the way we forgot they always were.

May God bless the whole world   June 3, 2013

I love the all-inclusive bumper sticker *May God Bless The Whole World,* which some awakened people created in reaction to the restrictive *God Bless America* bumper sticker. Not that I am against well wishes for this country, but I do not wish any other country any less than this one. The problem is the distinction between "them" and "us," whereby we believe that we are more deserving than "they."

As long as we exclude others from our well wishes, as long as we think we are better or more deserving, as long as we think of ourselves in isolation, we have a problem. My teenage son ran in a Spartan Race this weekend. It was hot, humid, long, and difficult. As a mother I of course worried and quietly asked for "the most benevolent outcome for his well-being and safety" (see Tom Moore's *The Gentle Way* for more on asking for positive outcomes). He was running with three of his friends. So it occurred to me that I wanted all of them to be well and safe as well, and I quickly added that. And then I thought, Gee, actually I would not want anyone in this whole race to be hurt—I really do want all racers to finish safely, and added yet another qualifier.

It is misinterpreted social Darwinian to think that one party has to lose for the other to win, or that there isn't enough well-being and goodness and abundance available for all of us. Win–win for all!

Death and wordlessness   June 13, 2013

Two days ago our dear sweet cat Snowball died, and I explained to my daughter how much we look at death from our human perspective. The regret and sadness and ensuing emotional heaviness in the chest all come from two things: our "word world," and a doubt that our existence could be more than just a once-and-never-again opportunity to appear on Earth, which of course causes a massive fear of death.

Existing in a "word world" enables us to live with awareness of the past and project into the future, but mostly prevents us from living in the present, as animals do (and as we did pre-language). We look back and remember, compare that to our present loss, and translate it into future loss. But the feeling of loss is one-sided because the transiting animal perceives the process totally differently. Animals are different from us because of their present-oriented consciousness and inability to reflect (although meditation and mindfulness teach us to enjoy fleeting moments of being in the moment).

I recently read a very helpful description of an animal's death in Martha Beck's *Finding Your Way In A Wild New World*. Beck reminds us that "we suffer more from our thoughts about events than from the events themselves. Detaching from our verbal thoughts eliminates almost all our psychological suffering."

"Death is the stripping away of all that is not you. The secret of life is to 'die before you die'—and find that there is no death," writes Eckhart Tolle

The blessing of food   *June 18, 2013*

My son and I picked up some things at Walmart the other day, and he reflected that the "Walmart atmosphere" with its blue-gray color scheme surely has a negative influence on their employees' psyche (I agree—I'd much rather work at Target for its warm color scheme). The *New York Times* recently reported how we adapt our behavior to whose company we are in—which means that we adopt and become part of the surrounding consciousness or frequency, that there is a fluid, seamless interrelationship. When I travel to France or Germany, I put on my French or German cultural hat, and I become a lot more French or German than I am here at home in the U.S.; when I am here, I am back to my (almost) American self (reminds me of mimicry in biology).

Masaru Emoto's astounding water experiments became known in the West through the 2004 movie *What the Bleep Do We Know?* The thesis of this movie is the seamless interconnectedness of the physical and the spiritual, the influence of consciousness on the physical, and the far-reaching consequences of this hypothesis (let's call it that, although I firmly believe in it).

Although not yet accepted by the scientific community (which in general doesn't yet accept that consciousness might influence, much less create, matter), Emoto's research of several decades indicates that consciousness influences the molecular structure of water. He maintains that we can improve the structure, or frequency, of water by taping a sign with a positive word to a water container, or imbuing it frequentially with spoken words, such as saying out loud "love" or "gratitude." Think about the benefits of a glass of water, if it had indeed absorbed such positive frequency, and think of the implications for the human body, which consists of between fifty and sixty-five percent of water.

All of this reminds me of the religious custom of blessing food and drink, which would improve its frequency or energy, and therefore its beneficial influence on us.

Smile, it's free   July 16, 2013

Not only is it free, as weekend workshop facilitator Cynthia Bianco said to us, it is also highly infectious. Try not to smile when someone smiles at you—it feels quite awkward. How often does it happen that someone smiles at you when you put on a stern face? When you smile directly at people, most can't help but smile back at you. And, lo and behold, the world becomes a friendlier place. Smiling immediately turns your energy around from negative to positive. They say, "Fake it 'til you make it." That's good advice, since body and mind are interconnected and influence one another. The more you gently remind yourself to smile the more it becomes part of an inner radiance.

One of the women who attend an energy development class I regularly go to struck me because she always has this radiant, contagious smile on her face. It makes the whole room shine, and it actually feels weird not to smile back.

Yesterday morning I had a chat with my daughter's camp van driver. On my way back to the car a worker, who was painting some woodwork on a store entrance, smiled at me spontaneously. I realized that I was still smiling from my conversation with the van driver, and that my smile spread outward like a ripple effect.

Try it sometime—walk down the street smiling and see what happens.

The sacredness of things   September 3, 2013

Mass production takes the sacredness and magic out of things. It makes them cheap. One-of-a-kind objects, like artwork or a handmade craft or knitted sweater, or an apple pie made from scratch, are infused with the imprint of the maker. Such an item has a totally different energy than say that cheap plastic cup with its advertising logo, which ends up first as a pencil cup (although, annoyingly, it keeps tipping over), or as a brush cup (the weight of the water keeps it standing), but then inevitably gets thrown away or at least recycled.

Why do you hesitate to throw away your high schooler's clay bowl made in third grade? Why can't I get myself to throw away the chocolate rose my son gave me in second grade for Mother's Day, and which has been sitting in our dining room cabinet for eight years now? Because these things are infused with significance and meaning.

But I am ruthless with cheap stuff we seem to collect—useless

Disney key chains (how many key chains do you need?), plastic Lei from some party long ago which lost their magic the morning after, too many t-shirts with logos and pictures advertising someone else's cause, plastic toys too ugly and cheap to save for future generations.

Buy less, buy thoughtful, or make it.

An attitude of gratitude   September 9, 2013

How about thinking of life as a gift, as author Charles Eisenstein suggests? What an extraordinary opportunity, what a biological coincidence, what a marvel that you find yourself incarnated in this body, in this place, and during these times which Harvard psychologist Steven Pinker has called the most peaceful on Earth yet (despite what the media coverage might suggest).

Think about this opportunity as a gift to experience life on this beautiful Earth, a gift to express your spiritual self in this three dimensional realm through all the things you do, a gift to share your life with all the people you choose to have around you. This perspective creates an attitude of a half full glass instead of a half empty glass, an attitude of gratitude, an attitude of joy, amazement, and wonder.

Research suggests that people with a positive outlook on life, a good social network, and a can-do attitude have a longer life expectancy. So from that perspective alone it's worth it. What if life were really only about the actual experience and joy of being?

Here's some magic   September 13, 2013

What about pragmatism? What about rational-analytical thinking and the glorification of science? What about pushing our emotions under the rug, or believing our Western culture to be superior to, or more evolved, than indigenous cultures? These beliefs are all a reflection of the loss of the spiritual, the loss of an appreciation for the mystical, the wonderment of life.

When I was little, Christmas was so full of glitter and magic and mystery. My sister and I would even climb into the attic in the middle of the year to open up the Christmas boxes and look at the sparkly ornaments to try to recapture some of that magic (but it works better when it's cold outside, the candles are lit, and it smells like cinnamon and cloves).

Life is so one-sided, so devoid of sparkle without this magic—so, well, *pragmatic*. But the magic is there, it's right in front of your eyes. Whether the sparkle of a Christmas ornament, the glistening of rain drops on a leaf, or the shiny beauty and perfection of red peppers in a bowl—it's really quite magical. It pays to tune into the magic because it's everywhere around you!

Finding the You in You   October 4, 2013

It's nothing new—that beauty comes from within, and that beauty also entails youthfulness. As Jane Brody explained in a recent *Times* article, you can lather yourself with all the creams in the world, dye your hair, tuck your tummy—if you are miserable, it shows. And if you are happy it shows also. The French word for the state of mind that makes you shine from within is *épanouie* — the best translation is *radiant*. Radiance shines through. When everything works well for you in life, when you are who you need to be (or working on it), and do what you need to do (or trying to get there), it goes way beyond manicured nails, or a breast or nose job.

I'm never so sure what women are trying to achieve when they dye their hair or otherwise tweak their external features (granted there are exceptions). After all, the world's oldest model, Carmen Dell'Orefice (she is eighty-two!), would no longer be Carmen if she dyed her signature white hair. She looks radiant and unique with it. And if Sofia Loren had had cosmetic surgery to make her into a standard Barbie beauty she would no longer be Sofia Loren. Her lips and eyes are so uniquely Sofia.

There is no one more unique than you! And all that is special about you will come out and shine and glow and radiate when you do that inner work. It's about finding the You in You.

Choosing your parents   October 18, 2013

I always think that a radically different perspective helps us adjust our outlook on things. The thought of choosing your parents might sound crazy to some or even many of you.

Do you have an axe or two to grind with your parents? We easily blame them for what they sent us into this world with, for what they did or didn't do. Looking at it from a different perspective helps. As my yoga teacher said recently, "Life is not about right or wrong, life brings you experiences and opportunities."

Think about your parents from that opposite perspective, not the one in which you are the victim, but the one in which you are the recipient of a valuable quality or trait, or ability or realization.

I have a lot to be thankful for from my parents. They have been lifelong learners and taught me to become a critical thinker. We lived in different countries when I was young, and so I learned to love traveling, discovering different cultures and how people do things elsewhere, and to explore and enjoy the different foods all these cultures have brought forth. On the other hand, I could blame them for not being very emotional or showing their deep love and appreciation for me enough (emotionally they are a bit "Northern"—you have to read between the lines).

But parents can also teach you by default, by *not* showing you love or acceptance, or whatever else you think you need. In that case their behavior may be making you aware of a quality you'd like to add to your life that is currently not there. You could turn your attitude around, and instead of blaming your parents for what they didn't give you, you could be grateful for making you aware of something you need that you are currently lacking. By default my parents have taught me to tell my children all the time how much I love and appreciate them, something my parents never openly expressed—although they are changing a bit as they are becoming older.

So what if you had chosen your parents before incarnating (oh, another radical thought) in order to learn and become aware of specific themes you need to work on? Just a thought. . . .

Never too late to tune in   November 12, 2013

I recently attended an orchid information and care workshop because I find those flowers so sculpturally beautiful. People have given me orchids in the past and I have tremendously enjoyed the long blooming (up to three months). However, the plants either did not survive at my hands, or if they did, they did not re-bloom. It did not sit well with me that I basically cared them to death and I thought I could do better, especially since people told me that they were pretty easy to care for.

Wake-up time it was. The solution was so simple, yet it hadn't even occurred to me. My mind had not been open; I had not tuned in. Now that I have, I've found out that the plants need fertilizer on a regular basis, besides water and light (and repotting every two years). Oh, boy! Food! The poor things had not received any food!

Wake-up time can happen anytime. It's a shift in thinking. But we can also promote it by tuning in, focusing on a particular area of interest or concern, and delving deeper. The answer will come, and then we wonder how we could ever not have considered this new view.

The first snow   December 9, 2013

We are home awaiting the first snow of the season (two to five inches, they say). When we lived in Manhattan, I used to love snow days (and nights) because the snow would muffle the city sounds, and the streets would become quiet, but also because the snow would cover all the darkness of the cityscape, all the dirt, with a pristine white blanket (at least for a short time).

Snow days are different now, but the essence is still the same. Snow days are happy days for children (of all ages—mine aren't so little anymore): They sleep in, lounge around in pajamas, and go out to play in the snow. For me it's still work but with the knowledge that I can't get out for a quick yoga lesson or some Christmas shopping, worrying that my hubby will get home safe (he only stays in if it's really bad), shoveling some snow with the kids, and then warming up with hot cocoa and playing Christmas music. Ah, and Christmas-card writing, a perfect day for it.

Snow days quiet the world down, slow our pace, beautify the brown-gray winter landscape. Snow days are a reminder to stop rushing and smell the roses (or feel the snow)—a gift from Heaven.

You are the center of the universe   December 13, 2013

"Life's not coming at you but from you," my yoga teacher said recently. This is something quite amazing to ponder because it turns the way we perceive ourselves in relationship to the world upside down.

We tend to have the impression that we are a victim, that people are there to make our life miserable, that stuff happens just to annoy us to no end. It's the blame attitude.

When we are in that mode everyone else seems responsible for our misery. Oftentimes I have waited at a party (where I don't know a lot of people) for someone to come up to me and start a conversation, in which case I didn't have such a good time. Recently I went to a function and just walked up to people, re- or introduced myself, and engaged in conversation. . .and lo and behold, I had a great time. I was the initiator of my experience, I made the good time happen instead of waiting for someone else to make it happen for me.

So back to this fantastic phrase—what you put out there comes back to you. When you put nothing out, nothing much comes back. In a way you are the center of the universe and it all emanates from you!

My child, my teacher   December 20, 2013

The traditional perspective was that children should be seen but not heard. Children are supposedly lesser people because they are young and inexperienced. Watching children these days I am occasionally wondering whether some parents are now sending the exact opposite message by permitting their children just about anything, showering them with material stuff, failing to teach them respect and social manners, worshipping them endlessly, and providing no gauge or boundaries—basically granting them adult style freedom. But I am headed elsewhere yet. I believe that we can actually learn from our children even though they are indeed much younger and have less life experience (on the surface).

First of all, young children especially react in a socially unfiltered way. They speak truthfully and to the point (refer to *The Emperor's New Clothes*), without trying to spare people's feelings. Secondly, from a spiritual perspective our children are our peers because we are all equal as spirit beings (in a material body). We could go further yet, into the idea of reincarnation. Here we get into potential role reversals and the possibility that your child might have been your parent, mentor, or partner in another lifetime. Intriguing.

When my daughter was ten we had a deep and spiritual conversation about defining health and healing, and how they were more a mental than a physical thing. And in conclusion she burst out, "Well, then, no one is healthy, not even a doctor."

Children can be downright wise. Next time your child says something that upsets or irritates you at first blush, do listen, completely, and try to see their side, where they are coming from. Often we think we know better, but sometimes they actually do.

New Year's resolutions   January 1, 2014

The Russian billionaire Mikhail Khodorkovsky came to two major philosophical-spiritual realizations during his ten years in prison. One of them is very relevant on this New Year's Day, when many of us make resolutions. Khodorkovsky said, "I think the Russian problem is not just the president as a person. . .the problem is that our citizens. . .don't understand that their fate, they have to be responsible for it themselves. They are happy to delegate it."

This is a life-changing realization for everyone who wakes up to this enormous and beautiful responsibility, because that is what it is. We can't wait for Prince Charming to show up at the doorstep with a million dollars. We have to show intent, move ourselves in the direction to where we want to go, and actually do it. It is work, it takes courage jumping over your own shadow, it means taking risks, and it may be uncomfortable at times. But it is rewarding and it works!

No diet pill or new fangled miracle diet will take your

pounds off for you if you are not willing to pull through with it. Complaining about the government and not voting, or taking action in your own small way, is delegating "we the people" to some abstract politician or entity, as Khodorkovsky pointed out.

With every New Year's resolution you need a solid action plan that comes from the heart; think business plan for whatever you are striving to achieve, whether it is losing weight, making more money, moving to a warmer climate, leading a more balanced life, or whatever else.

Let's toast to intent and courage, because they are what make things happen!

Let the universe work for you   January 3, 2014

There is a difference between pushing, pushing, pushing, possibly against a wall, and putting intent out there and letting the universe do the rest. Our son, who will go for his road test later this month, had been looking for a well-priced used car (a stick shift was a must) since the fall. At every for-sale vehicle by the roadside, we stopped—price too high, no stick, bad condition. Local dealerships were too high-priced, and there were no appropriate ads in the papers. He became frustrated, but I kept saying that there was no rush since he didn't even have his license yet, and once the time came closer we could make a more concerted effort to find him a car.

Well, through a comedy of unexpected circumstances we ended up going to his great-uncle's for Christmas, and lo and behold—we pulled up and found a car for sale in his driveway. Our son jumped out in excitement, looked at the car and the sign in disbelief, and announced that it was a stick shift and cost exactly what he had intended to spend.

Voilà, or That Was Easy!

It's your choice   *January 28, 2014*

Whether you look at your teacup as half full or half empty, whether you react to the grumpy cashier at the checkout line with compassion (she is having a bad day, who knows what happened at home), or send an angry signal right back at her with an irritated reaction—the choice is always yours.

Your reactions come from your beliefs. Every thought in your mind is a cause to an effect down the road. I mentioned in a recent post that researchers found that depressed people are depressed because they have negative thoughts; they do *not* have negative thoughts because they are depressed. That difference is crucial, because you can change your thoughts—once you are aware of them.

Once we accept the responsibility of our thoughts, and that they create our reality, we are no longer at their mercy. Telling your mind what to think or not to think is one of the things that meditation teaches. If you do not rein in your mind, it gallops away with whatever comes along—and that can create a reality that is out of your control and not to your liking. Or you can dig deeper and become aware of what you are actually thinking.

Think about it.

Creating meaning   *February 11, 2014*

We live in a lopsided material-scientific culture, in which much of the qualitative, spiritual-philosophical, unseen aspect of life gets shoved under the rug, at least most of the time.

So much of our life seems to revolve around rushing from one place to another, buying stuff and more stuff (more than we need), keeping up with the Joneses on techno gadgets and what not, stuffing our children's schedules with all sorts of activities in hopes of some advantage or other over all the other children running in the same direction of seemingly limited college spots, job spots, life spots, and spending a lot of time idling around on screened devices by ourselves, alone. Stop!

We try to stuff the gaping spiritual hole in our lives too often with money. But meaning does not come from stuff and money. The reason that no amount of money can ever be enough is that we use it to fulfill needs that money cannot actually buy. We try to buy excitement, pampering and love, recognition, validation, and—yes—meaning.

Yet meaning is something we create from nothing. Meaning is the qualitative aspect of life. We can find it in and with the people we surround ourselves with, and in the activities we chose to do with them (volunteer work, meals and get-togethers, church, our work, sports), we can find it in the activities we do on our own (our work, our hobbies, even our chores). Often we find it more when we give than when we receive.

So teaching, volunteering, inviting, helping, putting yourself out there, giving—those are meaningful and deeply satisfying activities, and they are free!

Heart stuff   February 14, 2014

"All spirituality is, is the path of the heart," says Marianne Williamson. On this Valentine's Day, day of love and day of hearts, let's remember that no amount of material things (diamonds, chocolates, or flowers) can replace true expressions of love.

Expressions of love come from an open heart. A few examples are speaking kind words you really mean ("You always look so pretty," or "I couldn't have done a better job"), empathetic gestures (a slight touch on the arm, a sweet kiss, a long warm look), encouragement ("I knew you could do this"), true compassion (being a good Samaritan), wanting to be of service ("May I show you how to do this?" or "Is there any way I can help?").

Opening your heart opens your mind and opens your life. So let's try to be a little spiritual today.

The nature of our dualistic world   May 6, 2014

Living twenty-five miles from a nuclear power plant (as the crow flies) makes me wonder sometimes. They always say that these facilities are safe—until they are not (think Three Mile Island, Chernobyl, Fukushima). There simply is no guarantee.

We live in a dualistic world. You may wonder what that is and what that has to do with it? The world we live in exists through its opposites, it exists as a juxtaposition of opposites with all the shades of grey in between. We would not be able to experience

dark without the existence of *light*, we are unable to define *love* without its opposite *hate*, we experience *sour* in comparison to *sweet*.

When we make a choice, when we vote for something, when we make something happen, inevitably its opposite is brought into existence. That is the way this world functions. We strive for safety. Actually, we think we can guarantee ever more safety with ever more refined technology. But that's a fallacy, it's a delusion.

When we vote *for* nuclear power, its positive and negative aspects will inevitably manifest for us. If we don't want to experience its negative aspects—nuclear meltdowns, contamination, radiation catastrophes—we must eliminate the use of nuclear power altogether.

When we vote *for* the death penalty, we must accept the horrendous reality of botched executions, such as the one in Oklahoma last week. The only way to avoid it is to abolish capital punishment altogether. If we decide that genetic engineering can make positive contributions to the world we must accept its negative flip side. There is no way around it. Think about it.

BeYOUtiful   June 13, 2014

Inauthentic living creates a lot of stress. Inauthentic living is going against your grain, it's doing things to please or impress others.

Authentic living is about leaving behind pretense. It's about being *You* instead of a composite of what your family, your partner, your culture, or your friends think you should be. Living authentically is about being true to yourself, about doing what your heart tells you to, about aligning yourself with source (God, spirit, your higher self, whatever you wish to call it), about that which is good for you. This let's the energy flow.

Every time someone says to you "you should," you are being shoehorned into their vision of you. Every time you say to someone, "You should," you are doing the same to someone else. A lot of times you probably tell yourself, reluctantly maybe, "I should," because of some preconceived notion or belief you hold. Think again.

I learned early in life to be different and to stand up for my beliefs. My best friend in elementary school taught me that lesson. She was different, she came from a different background than the mainstream kids, she looked exotic with her jet black hair and green eyes, and some kids made fun of her because of the way she spoke. I came to her defense, which in turn sprouted a fierce sense of individuality in me. Now I teach my children to critically inspect the many cultural mainstream paradigms before following the lemmings.

Many of us live in fear—of not having enough (money or other things, but mostly money), losing our job if we don't please the boss, losing our social standing if we do something outside of the social norm of our peers. Conforming for supposed emotional protection at the expense of authenticity is always a compromise.

Feeling good about who you are deep down takes courage because oftentimes that means going against what others do, think, or say. But it makes you shine. BeYOUtiful is what you want to be, because you become more beautiful the more you become *You*.

Receiving graciously   *August 7, 2014*

In a way, we all want to be loved and accepted and patted on the back for it. But being a supposed goody two-shoes and feeling guilty about accepting a present is misconstrued.

A while ago we gave a friend's daughter a money gift upon her graduation and received a thank-you card back with a note that read *You didn't have to do that.* I know that phrase. I have heard it often among family members, and it circulates widely. A few years ago I was playing money tag with my housekeeper. I paid her, she gave me some money back because she thought she had worked less than what I paid her, but then I stuck the money back into her purse, wanting to be generous. She finally put an end to our money tag and said something like, "You need to let people give to you." The Japanese have the complicated social custom of *giri,* a kind of reciprocal indebtedness incurred when giving a larger present.

Think about the feelings that come up for you when you get a present versus when you give a present, especially one that you have selected particularly carefully, or that took a long time to create. Oftentimes, I get more of a charge from giving, and seeing the surprise and pleasure on the receiver's face, than from receiving. But that twisted fact makes us so mutually intertwined that we need to become as gracious a receiver as being a gracious giver. Let others give to you and relish receiving.

Routine, glorious routine   *August 19, 2014*

Children are getting bored (although they say they love summer vacation and hate school), parents are getting antsy. Summer is waning, the local tomatoes don't get any better than this, it is high pesto time, and we are approaching Labor Day fast. Schools have sent out supply lists, the children are relishing their last days of endless sleep, laziness, and boredom, and we parents are enjoying the last days of no-school routine.

During the summer months bedtime was undefined and breakfast on your own, beds remained unmade, dinner was late, my yoga routine went bye-bye, and work came and went in spurts for me, unorganized and interrupted.

It is time to revert back to school day routine. For me that means getting up early to make school lunches for my teens, having a sit-down family breakfast, tidying the house and making the beds, before going about my work in peace and quiet, and one long undisturbed stretch until the afternoon, putting on lipstick every morning, organizing after-school activities, cooking dinner every night, and making sure there is a bedtime.

We need the looseness of summer to enjoy the rigor and organization of the rest of the year, and vice versa. They complement each other in a yin yang kind of way, the way weekend versus weekday routines do.

Scarcity is a state of mind   August 29, 2014

Whether you look at the grass patch in front of your house (so many grass blades), the sand on the beach (so many grains of sand), the stream in the woods (so many water droplets), or your neighbor's apple tree (how many apple seeds on one tree?—imagine all the new apple trees that could grow from all those seeds), or the stars in the night sky. Nature's abundance is limitless.

If Nature is so abundant, then scarcity (as in, "I don't have enough money," or "I don't have any friends," or "I have to hurry, otherwise they'll run out of fill-in-the-blanks") is a fabricated state of mind. Our mind is all powerful, and it influences how we see our world—and, yes, everyone inhabits their own version of the world. Since we exist in a continuous energy exchange with our surroundings the universe reflects back to us what we put out. If you keep looking out for lack, you will see lack reflected back to you. If you put out abundance, the universe reflects all that abundance out there back to you.

You may have heard of "gratefulness journaling," writing down moments of gratefulness during the day in order to become more content. In a similar way you can train yourself to become more aware of abundance in order to promote more abundance in your life. Be aware that writing things down is more powerful than just thinking them because this crystalizes your thoughts, it brings you one step closer to actual manifestation. So writing down when you become aware of abundance helps to set this thinking into your mind. Notice the abundance of sunshine outside, abundance of air, the abundance of bees, of carrots at the market, of cells in your body, of delicious moments in your life—imagine away and feel yourself expand.

How do you see things?   January 30, 2015

"We do not see things the way they are, we see things the way we are." That's a remark of potentially old and unknown origin, but has most often been attributed to the writer Anaïs Nin. What is it supposed to mean?

When we were young we all had those fears of dark basements, creatures lingering under our beds at night, or perhaps were afraid to bring the trash out after dark. We saw the world from our imaginary kid perspective, full of unknowns, of lurking dangers, of mystical creatures. When we became older those fears dissolved as a result of new knowledge, and we began to see the world from a different and new perspective, a more rational adult perspective.

Neither perspective is more real or less real, each is just one of many ways to see and experience the world. Imagine how a cat or a bee might experience this same exact world we live in? An Australian aborigine sees and experiences the world from his particular traditions and symbiotic connection with Nature.

It's as if the world wrapped itself around our particular beliefs and perspectives, and mirrored back to us what we put out and who we are. You've probably heard something like, "money begets money," or "the more love you give, the more love you get." You see and get more of what you keep putting out. When you believe in the beauty of the world and the beauty of people, your world will be beautiful. If you believe in abundance you will have plentiful. You see things the way you are.

Take a look around and notice what you see.

Act of random kindness   February 18, 2015

A few days ago I had to take my car back to the auto body shop to fix a small chip I had previously overlooked when they repaired some deer damage. When I came to pick up the car and pulled out my wallet they said, "No charge." I was floored. I had never before experienced an act of random kindness (although this wasn't entirely random) and was so surprised and grateful.

It was amazing how this little event lifted and improved my mood for the rest of the day. Don't underestimate the enormous influence, good and bad, you have on all the people you encounter during the day. Your attitude reverberates out and out because it not only infects the people you have direct contact with, but also influences those next down the line, and on and on. Imagine how much good a smile, a kind word, a helping hand, or a word of encouragement can do.

Gut feelings and hunches   February 24, 2015

Quite frequently I know who is calling as soon as the phone rings—and I am not cheating and looking at the caller ID. I am sure you have experienced a "hunch" or a "gut feeling" about something, maybe you have seen ghosts, or not. Maybe you trust what you have experienced and do something with that information.

But more often than not you probably ignore it and let it pass by because it doesn't seem real.

Because these experiences are invisible—you can't see that hunch, you can't grab that ghost—and we have become so visual to the exclusion of our senses beyond the fifth, we don't attach much importance to these experiences. Since the Age of Enlightenment our culture has discounted the senses that pick up this type of information (clairvoyance, clairaudience, clairsentience). Moreover, our culture has become increasingly fast, which makes it impossible to pick this stuff up without slowing down, being quiet and listening inward.

Just like animal tracks in the snow make raccoon, deer, and cat wanderings through our property visible and real in the winter, while we can only gather their presence with the help of clues at other times of the year (shaved bark, droppings), we can make this kind of ethereal information real and trustworthy through training our senses.

Hunches come to everyone differently, through your inner ear or eye or thought. Take notice next time whether it comes to you as a thought passing through, hear an inner voice, or perhaps see a picture of the caller popping up in your head. Simply pay attention and acknowledge it next time this happens. Confirm that the information you get is correct and acknowledge that as well. This strengthens your trust in picking this type of communication up so you can actually make use of it.

My daughter and I recently took a class in animal communication—animals communicate telepathically—and learned to tune into our cats and strengthen our ability to listen to, pick up, and get information to and from them. Our instructor explained that it is like learning a new language and requires practice, practice, practice. Just as when you decide to learn Russian or French, it doesn't happen overnight. Of course it seems a bit unreal at first because the cat sits there in silence and without facial expressions, while something is clearly going on in its mind. We have to go deep and inward to pick it up.

Next time the phone rings, why not try to guess who is calling?

You *do* have a choice   March 17, 2015

Oftentimes we don't realize that we have a choice, we simply react and do because we are on autopilot. But we *do*. We have a choice of *how* to react to someone or to something.

I was in a meditation class last night and another attendee explained how potholes make him very angry, and how they trigger the same reaction in him every time. He gets so mad at the authorities for not doing anything about springtime holes in the road. It is quite liberating to realize that you have a choice of how to react. You could of course become angry every time you encounter a pothole, but that becomes silly after a while, and it's not of much use. You upset yourself and the pothole doesn't improve. You could call up the authorities and make them aware of a particularly large and deep pothole that endangers other drivers as well (I did that a few years back and they actually filled that pothole pretty quickly). That is empowering—but you can't call up about every pothole. Or you could decide that you no longer wanted to react to that emotional pothole anger trigger and just let it go. So what? It's just a pothole, big deal.

Some choices are more painful than others. When our head struggles with our heart, and when the head wins and the heart loses, it creates even more pain. But the choice is still yours. Consider taking a deep breath before reacting to an emotional trigger person, your mother-in-law or perhaps the noisy neighbor, then remember that you don't have to react with anger, that it is your choice.

The ego is reactionary and wants revenge, but at what cost? Tit for tat of course. The higher self will say, "Forget about it, it's unimportant, let it go, forgive." That's a more freeing choice.

The past doesn't exist   March 27, 2015

In reality our existence is composed of endless consecutive Now moments, one after the other, and another, and another. We always exist in the Now, although our minds may be all over the place, spending a lot of time in the past and in the future.

But the past does not exist, nor does the future. The past is just an accumulation of memories that live in our mind, while the future is something we are creating right now in the Now, but that has not happened yet. The past was Now at one time, but now that it's gone it's only a memory and no longer real.

In our minds we keep thinking about experiences from the past and projecting them into the future, creating fears and worries. We anticipate and expect that unpleasant experiences from the past will be repeating themselves in the future (and the more we do, the more they may). So then we worry about the future, and strategize and plan to avoid that projection from happening. Hence, we live in our minds, which live in the past and in the future—which both don't exist. Crazy, right?

If we simply lived entirely in the moment, in the Now, and left that non-existent past, and that not-yet-created future alone, there would be no need for fears and worries. How great is that? Think about it.

Balancing act   May 5, 2015

Each yoga session is different for me. Some days I'm more flexible than others. Some days I balance better than others. The flexibility has more to do with the time of day—stiffer in the early morning, more flexible as the day goes by and I move my body more. The balancing ability, on the other hand, has everything to do with my state of mind, how balanced I am internally, how focused I am. Some days when I try to do tree pose I can only get my leg to ankle height, and still, I wobble and have to put my toe down periodically. Other days, as if by magic, I get my leg all the way up to rest against my thigh and I stand in suspended stillness.

The more scattered or agitated I am, and the less balanced my state of mind, the more difficult the balancing poses are. The more calm my state of mind, the better those poses work. Most importantly I find, is to let go of straining or willing myself to get somewhere. Instead, I pick a neutral focal point in mid-distance, maybe a nail on the wall or a light switch, and use this to keep focused on the pose instead of watching my thoughts galloping through my head. The less I strive to create a perfect tree pose, and simply follow wherever my body takes me, the better. Then it becomes like a meditation in action.

Passion for the cause   May 15, 2015

"If you want money because you're a good doctor, that's good. But if you are a doctor because you want money, that will kill a lot of persons," the filmmaker, author, and all-round artist Alejandro Jodorowsky said in a recent Chronogram interview.

They say that the money will come if you follow your passion. But many of us are in job situations we don't care about, are indifferent about, even hate. Many others, and I am one of them, hold two jobs—the money-making one (which I actually quite like), and the creative, passionate one (which I like even more, and would love to do more of). Those of us in creative fields such as writing, making music, painting, or acting have a bit of a harder time earning an honest living in a culture that is lopsidedly in favor of the money making and business aspect of occupations. But where would we be without art and creativity? It's the soul of life.

As an employer I realize how important proper casting is. It is just as much my responsibility to correctly interpret a candidate's abilities, character, and knack for the job s/he is applying for, as it should be the candidate's responsibility to be as open and honest as possible about herself. If an employee compromises her values or passion for money (it's just a job, I can pursue my passion on the weekend), it comes out in broad daylight very quickly.

When weekend is all you are dreaming about all week long, maybe it's time to realign with your true self and figure out a way to do more of what you love to do.

Let the universe do its job   June 23, 2015

It's probably happened to you that you misplaced your keys or your wallet. Or maybe your glasses. The other day my daughter was up in arms because she had misplaced her wallet with her library and debit cards in it. She looked everywhere but couldn't find it. So she came to see me and asked what she should do.

Some people pray to Saint Anthony, patron saint of lost items. I told her to send the universe a request to turn up her wallet before going to bed, or before six o'clock, or however else she wanted to formulate her request. "Then," I said, "let it go. Forget about it. Don't think about it anymore. Let the universe do its job."

Lo and behold, around six o'clock she came with a really big grin on her face and exclaimed, "I found it!"

This method also works for coming up with solutions to problems you have been banging your head against the wall about. When you try too hard, solutions from outside your usual frame of mind don't have a chance to penetrate the thickness of that mind wall. Side stepping the thinking mind is a much better way. Before going to bed put your problem out to the universe and state with intent that you'd like to wake up to a solution. Then let it go, don't think about it anymore, go to bed and see what comes up in the morning. The solution is likely to come from the place where we go when we meditate or daydream, and it may just be a really good one.

Try it sometime. And always, always, thank the universe.

No one likes to lose   June 30, 2015

According to our current cultural thinking if I want to win I have to take it away from you. Our economic culture of lack has conditioned us to think that there is not enough, that *you* have to have less if *I* want to have more. This thinking brought forth the survival of the fittest misnomer of how Nature supposedly works—although Nature is really a lot more complex and cooperative than that.

This belief system—and that's all it is!—has also brought forth a host of competitive games and sports that always create one loser and one winner. Imagine if we could all win? Imagine if no one had to lose? We wouldn't have to explain away our crummy feelings when we are losing with "being a good loser." Losing makes you feel crummy. No one likes to lose! Don't kid yourself or your kids.

The better way is called cooperation over competition, working out solutions that work for you and me, not just for me. It may require a concession, it may require my coming a bit your way or vice versa. But what's so bad about that if we can both win?

When we sold our house last year we had a price in mind we wanted to get. But the market said otherwise. We could have insisted, and sat on our house some more, and waited for that illusory "winning" sale. Instead, we went with the flow. We sold for a bit less, we sold exactly when we needed to, and we sold to the one buyer who really wanted our house—in the end we all won.

On forgiving   September 11, 2015

I find forgiveness incredibly important. Forgiveness is the key to avoid carrying grudge, resentment, anger, and all those other unpleasant, low-frequency feelings around with us, embedded in our cells forever.

It's not about forgetting what happened on this day, not about shoving it under the rug, but forgiving and overcoming helps to move forward. Stuck energy becomes stale. It feels good to let go and release. It makes you feel lighter. Like when you have cried your heart out, then sobbed some, then eventually the tears stopped flowing, and finally you were ready to take a deep breath.

It feels so cleansing, so calming, and a bit like a fresh beginning.

What makes me happy   October 2, 2015

Here are some of the things that make me content and happy: a sense of inner peace; feeling safe and protected; a sense of abundance and the knowledge that I have all I need; friendship and togetherness (very, very important) and being part of a network; giving and experiencing kindness; self-realization, or expressing myself through what I do, and what and who I surround myself with; giving and sharing; being appreciated and respected by others; when those around me are well and content.

Things that don't contribute to my happiness: A new car seems pretty irrelevant to my happiness (mine is pretty beat up and not very new, and is a fine means of transporting stuff and people around the way it is); expensive jewelry (wouldn't want to worry about it, bling is just as pretty); expensive name brands (waste of money, only feed luxury corporations, and their actual value is probably ten percent of what they cost).

Sure, if I won the lottery I'd go on safari in Africa. But I am perfectly happy not going on safari in Africa. Money can buy basic creature comforts but not happiness. I wonder what makes you happy?

Hearts in my life

This past weekend I had heart coffee in Vermont. Heart-shaped *crema* may be the thing, but since I don't drink much coffee I was happily surprised, and the sight made me stop in my tracks for a minute and smile.

Many years ago my husband gave me a heart rock that he had found on our property. I am still wondering whether Nature shaped it like that by pure chance, or whether someone actually carved it into a heart and then lost it in Nature for us to find. Two winters ago I took a picture of snow melting away in a heart shape, and during a walk in the woods I found a cut-away, heart-shaped branch.

I like patterns, coincidences, symbols, and synchronicities. All these hearts popping up in my life reflect back to me what matters most, they are little humorous reminders of life's goodness. They seem like a twinkle from Heaven. Have you noticed any patterns popping up for you?

Clutter outside—clutter inside?
November 14, 2015

Clutter and mess, or not? Clutter and mess promote creativity, they say, while neatness and tidiness are associated with conventionalism. Yet, according to *feng shui* principles, clutter and mess keep stale and stagnant energy around, whereas uncluttering and tidying up let fresh energy stream in and open up new possibilities.

The basement in our old house was definitely not a creative space any longer. It was stuffed to the ceiling with stuff, so much stuff that we ended up with duplicates and triplicates of tools and stuff because we couldn't find our stuff. We got rid of a lot of stuff when we moved. And as soon as we were in the new house my husband meticulously and methodically organized the carefully selected leftovers on shelving units and hanging organizers. Now it feels really good to walk into the basement and actually find what you are looking for, instead of rummaging around and walking back up in frustration because you couldn't find those pliers or screws you knew you had somewhere.

I always wonder about the connection between clutter in your mind and clutter in your home or office. Clutter also has to do with a fear of letting go—you never know when you might need that stuff. And *feng shui* has a lot to say about clutter and where you have it. I find cleaning up and uncluttering quite liberating because you can literally see clearly again.

Messiness, while in the act of creating something specific, has definitely its creative purpose. But some organization in your everyday life is not only useful but downright refreshing and even necessary (there—that fresh *chi* energy). Can't find that spice you wanted to use in your rub? Can't find that black sweater that goes with those green pants? Can't find that book you were just talking about with your friend? Time to make room, clear out, unclutter, organize, and get that fresh *chi* moving. I am convinced it clears your mind, too.

Making time work for you   March 8, 2016

Intent is everything because it puts forth a desired outcome. Instead of letting life take its course—*que sera, sera*—predefining what you want helps to transport you towards your goal. In time management this kind of intent can be very helpful. Time elasticity comes to play in time management. Setting a goal of what you want to accomplish within a certain timeframe sets the framework, after that let the universe help you. You need to be very clear, though, in stating what exactly you want to accomplish, and define the timeframe clearly. Putting it in writing, such as on your to-do-list, is better than just thinking it in your mind. An example might be, "I must get to the airport by one o'clock," or "I will finish answering all my emails from yesterday by ten this morning."

Give it a try. I know it works.

Say yes!   March 11, 2016

"The secret of change is to focus all your energy not on fighting the old, but on building the new," fictional counselor Socrates said in Dan Millman's *Way of the Peaceful Warrior*. This is profound and cannot be said often enough—I must have written several blog posts along those lines, all saying the same thing in different words.

The universe doesn't hear the word "no," it leaves it out, it simply ignores it; so do animals, people, and especially young children. Guess what they do when you say, "Don't jump around on the couch." Guess what your cat does when you keep saying, with a look, "Don't scratch that couch!" Guess what you do when the boss says, "Don't do it this way." You'd rather not listen, because it doesn't feel good to be criticized. Besides, the boss didn't define how he actually wanted it done. But guess what you do when the boss says, "That report was written just the way I wanted it. Thank you for a job well done." You listen, you acknowledge, and you do more of the same, because you love being praised and praise feels good.

So when it comes to anything, be it children's behavior, employee behavior, your own health, life, define clearly what you want, not want you *don't* want, and move in that direction. Move forward instead of looking backward. That way you get more of what you want because the universe gets it.

Chaos or not
April 19, 2016

Nature can seem messy and disorganized. Gardening, for example, is not Nature, because we impose our sense of order on that little landscaped piece we call garden or backyard.

When our life is turned upside down due to sudden change or upset we perceive it as chaotic because the order and patterns we have created are undone. "Chaos is order without predictability," my yoga teacher so wisely said recently. The universe has laws, Nature has patterns, but we don't always understand or see them from our down-in-the-trenches perspective. When things become unpredictable we call them chaotic. Change can seem scary because we wade into uncharted territory; sometimes the light at the end of the tunnel remains very dim, or even invisible for some time. We wish for control and certainty because change requires us to shift, think differently, get out of our comfort zone, change patterns and ways of doing things.

But chaos and confusion can also be seen as full of opportunity, like a pregnant pause, a nudge from the universe to rearrange things. In hindsight, messy upsets usually and eventually reset themselves into new patterns that make sense once again.

Sometimes we just have to trust the universe for being *way* ahead of us and seeing the bigger picture.

Going on an adventure
May 3, 2016

I find it really important to get periodically out of what I'm in. Seeing the same people, doing the same things, following the same routines, reading the same kinds of books, not only gets boring but also keeps you in the same mindset. Creativity arises out of fresh inspiration. That's why we travel, take a pottery or ballroom dancing class, or anything else that's a bit out of our comfort zone, just for giggles. Key here is "out of our comfort zone." It's about building some new brain synapses. It'll always be more comfortable to stay home and relax, aka veg out. But going on an adventure is energizing.

This past Sunday the weather was miserable, it was actually pouring, and I was recovering from a bad cold. A good day to stay in, right? But we had tickets to two dance performances at the Fisher Center for the Performing Arts at Bard College. So we went. Lo and behold, I was so glad we went, for so many reasons. First of all we got to see Frank Gehry's architectural masterpiece. Second, we watched two zany contemporary dance theatre performances unlike anything I had ever seen before, one of them unanticipatedly participatory. Third, we discovered the teeny tiny, cute and trendy town of Tivoli. Fourth, someone in Tivoli gave us a recommendation for the nicest restaurant we ended up for dinner. Fifth, I came back feeling way better than in the morning, more energized, and totally inspired—and I still draw from it.

Moral of the story, sometimes you've got to pull yourself up by the boot straps and go off on a limb. You'll never know how much of life you miss out on if you don't get out of bed and live it.

What will be your future? May 13, 2016

Many people still have a hard time believing that their thoughts create the world around them, their experiences, even their afflictions. But look around you, look at your friends, look at the place where you live, look at the stuff you own, look at your job and your hobbies. Haven't you created all of it? If you have a beautiful garden, you love gardening and you created it. If you have a negative friend and don't appreciate her, reflect on why that person is in your life, then make a decision. It's your intentions, your efforts, your thoughts and beliefs, what you did and did not do, what you did and did not think and believe, that is reflected in the world around you, individually and as a culture.

If you don't like what's happening with the environment you need to do something about it on a personal level, change apathy and acceptance to thoughtfulness and action. If you don't like what you see, if you don't like what and who you are, dig deeper to uncover why and how you have created what you have created. Inspect the underlying beliefs and thoughts that went into it. It takes some work, and it might be tedious. But who said it was easy?

Today's thoughts create your future. If you think the same thoughts today that you thought yesterday your future will look like today. If you don't like today you need to change your thoughts and beliefs today to create a different future.

So what would you like your future to look like?

A kick in the butt   July 8, 2016

Sometimes I need a kick in the butt. I don't need to be hit over the head. But some recent work shenanigans rattled me profoundly out of my self-induced writing slumber and inspired me to get my book edits finally to the finish line, pretty fast, just like that. That was easy! Book done, off to test readers. After final suggestions and edits I'll figure out the publishing part.

It's easy to fall into complacency. When things are just too comfortable, too easy, then we stop learning, stop creating, stop being truly enthusiastic and excited about new horizons, new prospects, and new possibilities.

Of course you can get off your butt before then. It's less painful for sure. Be proactive and on your toes, anticipate the need for change before the universe helps you along, gently or not so gently.

A sense of community   July 29, 2016

Much research has been conducted on the positive influence of a good social network. In a nutshell, good friends are much more important to happiness than money, and even promote longevity. That is also one of the big messages we took away from our recent trip to Alaska.

We spoke to many non-indigenous people who had chosen to come live in this unforgiving territory for the love of Nature and the majestic outdoors. Distances are enormous, the state is sparsely populated, it's Nature over culture, and winters can be dark and lonely. Yet, the common thread in our conversations was community. Time and again people said that one of the reasons they love living in Alaska is the strong sense of community.

Friends are so important when there are no restaurants around, no movie theatres, no libraries, no cultural events. You rely on friends and neighbors for entertainment, especially during the long dark winter months. So people get together for tea, for knitting, for story telling, for potlucks, for helping to repair things, to go shopping together, you name it—any excuse is good to get together.

All the world's a stage   August 10, 2016

A few nights ago we saw Shakespeare's *As You Like It* on a beautiful outdoor summer stage. In this comedy Jacques famously says to Duke Senior, "All the world's a stage, and all the men and women merely players." This phrase reminds me very much of one of the interpretations of our earthly existence.

One of the ideas out there is that life is sort of a school, a learning experience through which we have the chance to better ourselves. But that idea leads to the thought of punishment for not learning one's lesson well. Another idea is that God/Spirit/Nature fragmented itself from Oneness into many, so that the One might know itself better. In other words God/you/I/We all are at the same time One, but split into all the individual beings to know itself/ourselves. In that interpretation we are actors and director on our own stage at the same time.

This is an amazing view that permits a bit of distance from the play. As director I can watch the play in amusement or dismay, and know a part of myself that I have forgotten. If I am sitting in the director's chair I get to steer life. I can see myself in others, as I would look into a mirror. As the actor I experience the joys and pains of life directly. So clever that Shakespeare built this deep wisdom into one of his delightful comedies.

It's all in the experience — August 26, 2016

We need to experience it to believe it, to feel it, to be alive. That not only includes what we would label "positive" or "enjoyable" experiences, but also what we call "negative" or "painful" experiences. As English poet John Keats wrote, "Nothing ever becomes real till it is experienced."

I can't truly know poverty from reading accounts of what it means not to know where my next meal comes from. I can't truly know unconditional love until I have had children that I fiercely want to protect from all the painful things that could possibly happen to them. I can't truly know passion and joy from reading a book or poem.

Humanity in its entirety is living this quandary in real time as we observe climate change. There are many who don't believe that this is actually happening, or who'd maybe rather stick their head in the sand, even though scientists have predicted it for several decades, and now have unfailing supporting statistics. We don't necessarily want to trust theoretical expert advice and scientific projection. It seems that we must feel the heat and the weather disasters, and the droughts and species reductions, before we are willing to act and say, "That is something I *don't* want, now that I have experienced it myself."

Chef Dan Barber expressed this in a documentary I recently

watched about his difficult beginnings. His take on adversity in life is that it teaches us where we *don't* want to go back to; and by default it teaches us what we want instead.

Take any recent experience and reflect back on it. Did it show you something that you would want to experience again? Did it show you something that you would *never* want to experience again? Did it teach you something that you want by showing you its opposite?

So much magic   September 7, 2016

Your heart beats about four thousand times an hour. Your digestive system does an amazing job digesting all the food you ingest, and distributing its energy for your use—all by itself, no assistance needed, no strategizing needed. Your body sweats when you work out, all by itself. Your lungs breathe, all by themselves.

Yet we are not machines, not engines, not computers. And some people want to tell me that there is no spirit behind it? No purpose? No absolutely, totally amazing life force? No higher purpose? In light of all that magic I simply can't subscribe to a strictly scientific-material worldview.

What's it all about?   September 9, 2016

What are some of the things you really enjoy in life? Do you get enough of those moments? Are you doing anything to get more of those moments? What could you do to experience more of those moments? Do you think you deserve more of those moments? Would you like to live more of those moments? What prevents you from having more of them?

Imagine what it would be like to have a life full of beautiful moments. Go for it.

It's the twinkle in the eyes   September 16, 2016

Have you ever noticed that His Holiness the Dalai Lama always looks like he is smiling? He always has a twinkle in his eyes. Eliezer Sobel wrote, in *The 99th Monkey*, a very humorous account of his search for enlightenment, "I opted for the teacher with the biggest twinkle, which I still believe is a very good gauge of spiritual teachers."

He hit the nail on the head. The twinkle in the eyes is it. It's what you acquire when you reach inner peace, when compassion flows through you, when your fears no longer get the better of you, when you are content, when you are comfortable being You, when you've got nothing to prove and everything to give, when everything is the way it's supposed to be, and when you no longer take yourself too seriously.

That's what I want.

The importance of rhizobia   September 23, 2016

I'm not much of a fiction reader but I just finished Barbara Kingsolver's *The Bean Trees* and enjoyed it a lot. The story conveys what I keep saying, that life is all about relationships. And life is all about relationships because life is about experiencing love in its many forms, as well as through its lack and absence. The Bean Trees' metaphor for this realization is the wisteria vine, whose root system attracts rhizobia, small bugs that attract nitrogen to the roots and assure the wisteria's survival even in poor soil. Bug and wisteria live in a mutually beneficial and interdependent relationship. One cannot survive without the other.

We may think that we can go it alone, get off the grid and be self-sufficient, but Nature is not like that. Nature is an entirely interdependent and mutually beneficent, inter-relational web of support that we humans are an integral part of. The more we care for each other, the more we enjoy love, life, and happiness.

We go to restaurants every once in a while and enjoy the experience. But what we enjoy a whole lot more is having people over or going over to friends' homes and sharing good food and good conversation. It costs a whole lot less and it cultivates relationships.

That's what it's all about.

The fox's secret   September 27, 2016

You may have heard it said that we need to drop from the head to the heart, or that the mind sometimes gets in the way. But what does that actually mean? Antoine de St. Exupéry's *The Little Prince* is a philosophical chef d'oeuvre full of great quotes. One of my favorites, the one that hangs on my fridge, is this one, "It is only with the heart that one can see rightly. What is essential is invisible to the eye."

When it comes to decision making, our rational-analytical mind sidesteps our feelings and decides strictly with the head, the left side of the brain, the math and science side. It foregoes checking in with the heart. Initially, we may believe that that's wise, and when solving a math equation it's essential. But in many instances our heart, our feelings, provide complementary, and sometimes contradictory information to the mind, that is valuable to consider, and can be really helpful—the "seeing rightly" part of the quote.

We can't see emotions and feelings, they are "invisible to the eye," yet they are essential to our human condition. We have all made mind based decisions we have regretted later on because we disregarded the heart, so keep the fox's secret in mind, or rather in your heart.

Letting go

Maybe fall is a good time to let things go, the way trees let go of their leaves before going into hibernation, a period of rest and internal renewal (that pregnant pause full of potential), before starting fresh again in the spring. I saw this beautiful quote by an unknown author the other day, "Autumn shows us how beautiful it is to let things go."

I love the fall for many reasons—the change of seasons and that getting-back-to-cozy feeling (just put on the flannel sheets), the fantastic colors, those delicious fall spice combinations and the wonderful festivities, but also the blusteriness of the weather, which feels like a giant sweep-up and cleansing.

The song "Letting Go," featured in the animated movie *Frozen*, became a huge hit a few years ago. Letting go of fears is liberating and makes you feel lighter. Fears cause us to put up barriers, put on figurative masks, hide our true feelings, and conceal who we really are. They also cause us to hold on to things that are no longer useful, like grudges, ill will, and all that pettiness that weighs us down.

Consider fall's metaphor of the beauty of lettings things go, letting it drain out of you, giving it up if it no longer serves, or weighs you down with emotional ballast—no need to hold on.

What a great day

It's pouring, it's blustery, the wind is driving the rain against the windows, and I'm loving it. Great day to sit at my computer with a cup of hot tea and get some work done. I don't have to feel guilty about not going out in the sunshine—none in the forecast. I can simply plug away in the coziness of my office and thoroughly enjoy this lousy weather from inside the warm house.

You can complain about the weather, but in the end it's all about attitude and outlook. Same weather, different perspective.

On the creative impulse   December 2, 2016

This is one of the many precious observations I found in Deepak Chopra's recent book *The Future of God*: "Nature exists to show us the full range of life in its most creative and most destructive forms."

It is horrible, heart wrenching, terrible when we witness or experience destruction and suffering. It hurts emotionally when a friend simply gets lambasted for her opinion. Chopra's phrase provides a lot of food for thought on offering an explanation for all the hatred, violence, disasters, and simply unpleasant experiences we encounter as we navigate life.

However, the bad stuff could be a point of inspiration for what we *don't* want, and in turn can become an incredible source of creative energy and renewal and impulse.

Imagine all the good stuff you want in your life that the bad stuff helps you to define. As in the yin-yang symbol, good and bad, disastrous and joyful, destructive and creative, are two aspects of the same whole, and exist through definition of their opposite.

If you don't like being out of a job, if you didn't like the result of the recent election, if you don't like your local politics, if you don't like the idea of killing animals for human consumption, if you don't like drab colors—turn that energy around and create what it is you actually want. Imagine the job you are looking for, vote in every and all elections (not only the presidential one), become active in your local community to improve its quality of life, eat more plant based foods, and surround yourself with lots of joyful colors.

Dwelling on the negative makes you depressed, complaining and whining is not effective. But turning a negative experience into a jumping point for something new and better is creative and wise. Just imagine!

2016 resolutions   December 29, 2016

Oh those fashionable New Year's resolutions. Do you make them? Do you keep them? Do you drop them? Yesterday, while in Manhattan, I was interviewed on the street by a Japanese TV station about New Year's resolutions. I told them that I don't make them, and that the success rate of keeping to them isn't terribly encouraging.

According to the Statistic Brain Research Institute about half of Americans make them, and about half of those maintain them for the first half of the year; thirty-nine percent of people in their twenties achieve them, while only fifteen percent of people over fifty do.

All of that doesn't mean that I am without gumption and don't have goals. It's just that I don't feel I need to wait until December rolls around to make a plan, although better in December than never. In order to stick to a resolution you have to make it a habit, and a habit builds after about a month of doing something regularly. And the resolution has to have a deep and long-term meaning so it's still attractive come February or March.

Another piece to the success of any resolution is some kind of a contract with yourself so that you cannot back out so easily. You might announce your plan out loud to some family members or friends. That way it becomes more difficult to pull out than if you kept it to yourself. Or reward yourself for sticking with it. Earlier this year I absolutely wanted to finish the third-to-last chapter of my upcoming book and I love shoes. The contract with myself was that I got to buy a new pair of shoes once I finished that chapter. It got done pretty fast!

Let's dream   January 17, 2017

A day late, but never too late for this message. While Martin Luther King, Jr. was a person of color, his message of love and peace and respect is of course universal, and has nothing to do with skin color. On Martin

Luther King Day we celebrate his courage in the face of hardship, his vision to communicate peacefully in a world fraught with adversity and strife, his vision for harmony and kindness on Earth, and for showing us a better way —a dream still, but let's keep dreaming.

Let's embrace his message in our own backyard—in our families, among our friends, at work, at school. When I can see myself in all other fellow men, in *any* fellow man or woman, when I can see that they all have the same needs for safety, a roof over their head, a good job, healthful food, dignity and respect, as I do, that they all have the same fears I do, and the same need for love and acceptance, skin color is no longer the issue.

When we become peaceful internally we will become peaceful externally. Let's all remember his dream and make it ours—it's a universal dream.

Why we need stories   January 27, 2017

Everyone likes a good story. We like to be transported, and we like to be entertained. Time stands still when I get lost in a great novel with a cup of tea by my side.

But stories can do so much more than entertain us. They can provide a mirror for something we go through or need, like when we commiserate with the heroine, or long to experience what she goes through. Then the story provides emotional support. Stories inspire us to muse and ponder and philosophize, perhaps to see things differently, perhaps to stretch our imagination and mind.

Another very important aspect of story telling, of creating a narrative, is to knit a culture or events together, creating meaning, making sense. Not all of us can see a pattern when we are walking through the woods and seeing all those individual trees. But once someone flies a drone above the trees, or climbs on a tower, so to speak, and sees the whole of it as a forest, sharing that narrative helps all of us to see the bigger picture.

Creation stories ground a culture in a narrative base. Cultural beliefs are a story that informs how people think about something (that mainstream medicine thinks of the body in a mechanical way is a narrative that informs our healing methods; when we change the narrative, the healing methods will change too). Traditional fairytales teach us about good and bad, and that light always triumphs over darkness. Without stories things seem random and our human mind needs patterns.

Nature changes all the time and doesn't need patterns, at least not human patterns of orderliness. We do. We create meaning and context through stories and narrative.

Quandary of choices   February 24, 2017

I have so many different types of tea in my kitchen cabinet—soothing green *sencha*, earthy green barley popcorn *genmaicha*, perfumy black Earl Grey, and strong basic Irish Breakfast, soothing chamomile tea, astringent rosehips and hibiscus, herbal bitter orange, and stomach calming fennel tea. Each tea has a different characteristic, which I drink according to my different moods, some are therapeutic, some are soothing, some have oomph, some have caffeine, some not. This diversity in teas is wonderful and offers me all these different options.

In general, we welcome choices like these, whether in food and drink, or the way we dress, or about the books we like to read. People, too, are diverse. So many different beliefs and convictions, so many different talents, so many different physical characteristics, and so many different expressions. Why is it then that we can sometimes feel threatened by the diversity in people? That we feel intimated by a different physicality, by a different opinion? Why do we feel safe among people who think like us? Why do we have a tendency to judge different opinions?

How about relishing our diversity? What do you think?

Why live deeply   April 25, 2017

Living deeply is about creating a meaningful life. It's about putting the quality back into life by creating win-win scenarios. This requires a shift in values, away from "profit above all," quantification, and our usual win-lose scenarios, to a value-based culture that is cooperative, sustainable, compassionate, and transparent. It's about creating a good-for-all, not just a good-for-some, culture.

Any reason not to want this?

Writing to learn   June 9, 2017

My daughter used to play teacher and explain her school lessons to an invisible audience while writing on her dry-erase board. It was a way for her to integrate her school lessons from the day and understand them better.

It seems that we teach best what we need to learn, or that we like to explain what we need to understand, or that we learn better if we teach what we're trying to understand.

Understanding is a process that solidifies through teaching or writing, hence the idea of homework or writing papers in college.

I am currently reading the book *Learning By Teaching*, which is chock full of relevant quotes. Author Donald Murray writes, "Why do writers write? . . .most of all to discover what they have to say." Brilliant! He goes on to quote novelist E.M. Forster, who said, "How do I know what I think until I see what I say?" and poet Cecil Day-Lewis, who concluded that, "We do not write in order to be understood, we write in order to understand." All these quotes express how understanding unfolds and deepens through processes such as writing or teaching.

Murray even takes this realization one step further when he says that "writing is an individual search for meaning in life." We writers discover the meaning of our own life through writing; writing for us is a process of self-realization in the same way that painting is a process of self-realization for an artist, or baking pastries is a process of self-realization for a *pâtissier*.

Life is a process, life is self-realization—through interaction with people and things. We each chose to live, to be life, through the lens of a particular medium—for the painter the medium is his art, for the writer it is her books. What is your medium?

So serendipitous   *June 27, 2017*

Serendipity is my new favorite thing in life. "The occurrence and development of events by chance in a happy or beneficial way," is how the Oxford Dictionary defines it. Serendipity seems to occur the more we refrain from trying so hard, from steering life too much. Oftentimes I want something specific for lack of better imagination, or for lack of courage to imagine something bigger and better yet. But when we try to will a predictable outcome we actually discourage the universe from bringing us the best of its abundance and fabulousness, we put the brakes on, we choke the energy.

I just love it when the universe brings forth something unexpected that is way better than what I could have envisioned on my own. Both our children found their first cars in completely serendipitous ways; exactly when they needed them, for the price they could afford, from people we could trust. In the spring the perfect, paid summer internship in Europe manifested for our son out of nowhere. And recently the possibility of producing a documentary from my book came about—something that was completely outside of my realm of imagination.

When things like these happen my enthusiasm bubbles over and I am in awe of the amazingness of the world. How have *you* experienced serendipity?

Ruminations
on growing food

Sacred agriculture   March 1, 2013

Agriculture is only about ten thousand years old and it has shaped today's cultures fundamentally. Agriculture enabled population growth and the population explosion of the past fifty years. Agriculture is also what has brought forth "culture" as we understand it—it is specifically agriculture that enabled the development of the first great cultures in Mesopotamia and Egypt. Agriculture was a new concept then, as we moved from a nomadic lifestyle, and collecting our food through hunting and gathering, to settling down and harvesting food from the same surrounding area year-in and year-out. The hunter-gatherer lifestyle permits Nature to renew itself naturally, while agriculture, if not practiced wisely and in tune with Nature, depletes the soil—and then what?

Agriculture is the unification of Nature and man. We exhibit our current disconnection from Nature through the type of agriculture we have created—soil-depleting monocultures that require outside chemical input to produce food at the expense of environmental and human health. However, the significant growth of the organic (funny—until about one hundred fifty years ago *all* agriculture was organic), sustainable (better than organic), and biodynamic (the best) agricultural movements demonstrates an emerging awareness of the deep connection between ourselves, Nature, and our food supply.

We exist as part of Nature, not *apart* from Nature, and strictly on the basis of light and water. Without Nature we do not exist. Sacred agriculture!

Cheap seeds or not?   March 11, 2013

I used to buy cheap seeds on sale at the end of the season, the cheaper the better, and non-organic of course. I didn't think it mattered whether seeds were grown organically or not. My somewhat limited belief was that if the vegetables grew without chemicals and in my own healthy soil, that was enough. But that is a narrow perspective.

Then I learned that poor soil (the depleted kind that needs to be sprayed chemically) makes poor seeds with poor genetic material, which in turn will make poor plants (and poor food). Or the other way round, mineral rich soil makes genetically complex seeds and plants that make for good food.

More recently I read an article by Margaret Roach that opened my mind to two more implications of buying non-organic seeds. First, "growing vegetables for their seed often involves more chemical use than growing those same crops for food" (didn't know that). Second, plants grown from non-organically grown seeds, adapted over many seed generations to exist in chemically enhanced soil, may not do as well in mineral rich and chemical free soil (didn't know that one either). Tom Stearns, founder of High Mowing Organic Seeds, says that, "Organic gardeners are using a dull tool when they use seeds from conventional agriculture."

Spiritual farming   April 19, 2013

Huh, you might ask? Yes, there is such a thing, and it is called biodynamic farming. The Biodynamic Farming and Gardening Association's website defines it as a "spiritual-ethical-ecological approach to agriculture, food production and nutrition."

Fred Kirschenmann, author of *Cultivating an Ecological Conscience*, explained in his 2010 keynote address at the association's conference that the present big-ag paradigm of maximum efficiency is geared towards short-term gain, and is only possible through specialization and simplification (the small picture, immediate gratification). However, he says, farms need to be run more like organisms (the Gaia principle), in sync with Nature.

We need a new agricultural paradigm, what with the bees

dying, crop varieties diminishing (Tom Standage reports that, "of the 7,100 types of apple [!] grown in America in the 19th century. . .6,800 are now extinct." *Wow!*), monocultures that discourage insect and bird variety and promote disease, and GMOs and pesticides as misguided solutions to increasing production with short-minded profit in mind. While there is so much more to say about the deficiencies of the present paradigm, I'd rather look towards the future and better solutions.

Organic agriculture, sustainable agriculture, permaculture, and biodynamics are all promising alternatives, of which the first is the most profit and least Nature oriented. The term permaculture comes from the contraction of permanent and culture and agriculture (there is indeed no culture without agriculture). Permaculture is a completely sustainable agriculture, practiced in symbiosis with local conditions and without waste. Biodynamics incorporates more lofty principles. Just like permaculture, it works with the farm in a symbiotic, wasteless, cyclical, organism-like relationship. In addition, it takes into account our embeddedness in the larger cosmic picture, and considers the planetary influences on seeds, crops, and soil, and works with "homeopathic" soil enhancements since the health of the soil is first and foremost in growing mineral-rich produce, the ultimate aim of agriculture: healthy soil = healthy food = healthy body.

Food forests   *June 21, 2013*

Permaculture, although around since the 1970s in Australia, is still fairly new over here. The word is a contraction of the words *permanent, agriculture,* and *culture* (interesting that *agriculture,* which means cultivation of the land, is so tightly tied to *culture*—without agriculture there is no culture!).

The idea of permaculture is a completely sustainable agriculture, and more so culture. Sustainable means that there is no "garbage," that everything we need to live on comes and goes in a permanent, circular, mutually beneficial and dependent, and therefore wasteless cycle. The principle of agricultural permaculture is planting crops together that complement one another in a wildly complex and diverse composition that emulates Nature, although it is man-made. These food forests work at every stratum of the vegetation, from low down mushrooms, herbs, and flowers, to the next level of berry and hazelnut bushes, to higher up fruit and nut trees.

This is not a new concept, though. But then—sometimes we need to revisit old ideas from a fresh perspective and a higher perch. Thanks to the suggestion of a friend, I recently read the book *1491* by Charles Mann and learned about *milpas*. Milpas are South American planting compositions that comprise up to a dozen crops (maize, avocados, squashes and beans, melon, tomatoes, chilis, sweet potatoes, jicama, amaranth, and *mucuna*), which all "complement one another nutritionally and environmentally." Some *milpas*, I learned, have been in existence for four thousand years without depleting the soil!

One of the problems of our conventional farming methods, exacerbated in monocultures, is the lack of diversity in crops, because a lack of diversity in the insect/grub/bird population follows from it. This disconnect between agriculture and Nature then depletes the soil on top of it all.

I am never advocating a return to the past! However, new for the sake of new is often short sighted. In this case we have several inspirational and sustainable agricultural models whose principles are worthwhile knowing about.

The whole kit and caboodle   May 27, 2014

Two recent articles made me aware of a truer meaning of *sustainable agriculture* and where we need to go next in our farm-to-table awareness.

The first one was about the enormous food waste in the E.U. created by discarding produce that doesn't look perfect, even though it is in good condition and tastes just like its more conformist looking counterparts. A young Portuguese woman started a produce cooperative named *Fruta Feia*, or Ugly Fruit, to market and sell such imperfect produce at twenty to thirty percent less.

The other article was from chef Dan Barber on widening the premise of sustainable agriculture and including in our food choices also those crops that are typically used as cover crops to replenish the soil. Soybeans, kidney beans, or cowpeas (used as animal feed) are typical nitrogen replenishers for the soil. But Barber was talking about a much more sophisticated and complex crop rotation that is needed to keep the soil fertile and full of minerals, which guarantees not only superior taste but also mineral and trace element rich foods (less supplements you'll need to take). Such other crops might include rye, barley, or buckwheat, all little used in this country because less marketed and less known.

Sustainability, in agriculture and elsewhere, is about a wasteless circular process, in which all "waste" becomes a reusable base component for the next process in the circle, thereby eliminating the idea of "waste" altogether. A sustainable farm would not buy outside fertilizer, seeds, and pest management products, instead using the farm animal manure for fertilizer, crop rotation, crop variety, and inter-planting as main pest control techniques, and saving its seeds from one year to the next. Being able to sell its cover crops in addition to its main crops makes the farm more viable and eliminates further waste.

The whole idea behind truly sustainable agriculture is to embrace every part of the agricultural process, the whole kit and caboodle, whether it's the little used rye (here in the U.S. at least), the funny looking strawberries, the carrots with a nose or legs, or the lesser known fava beans (I made a fava bean hummus the other day that was as delicious and tasty as a chickpea hummus).

When to sow and harvest   June 24, 2014

While native inhabitants, intimately knowledgeable about their local soil and weather conditions, have oftentimes known to plant in harmony with the lunar cycles, Maria Thun, a leading authority on biodynamic agriculture, took this idea one step further. She did extensive research on the planetary influences on all produce growing phases.

Biodynamic agriculture has often been criticized by skeptics. However, as it is dawning on us that the type of agriculture we have been practicing for the last fifty or so years may be doing more damage than good on a long-term basis, all kinds of alternative models are being resurrected and researched. These models all require a deep knowledge of local conditions—weather, soil, and native plant combinations. So it behooves us to be open to all kinds of old and new, gentle and co-creative ways to grow our food.

So back to where I'm headed, which is a more connected way to grow your veggies, and when. Based on her research, Maria Thun came to the conclusion that different planetary phases influence the growth of plants in different ways. She came up with optimal timings for sowing certain types of plants, depending on whether they are root based (i.e. beets, carrots), leaf based (i.e. kale, spinach), fruit based (i.e. tomatoes, eggplant), or flower based (i.e. marigolds), and when best to harvest.

You can buy the annual illustrated biodynamic Stella Natura calendar, which is easy to read and use and has many interesting articles, but a very consumer friendly version is also available online.

It has been demonstrated that produce grown in healthy, rich soil and sown according to this calendar makes for a much stronger and more resistant plant (I would also recommend buying organic heirloom seeds, instead of the conventional kind) and a more prolific harvest. Give it a try.

Organic soil and flowers?   September 26, 2014

A lot of people are now aware of the notion of growing food organically. But did you know that there is organic potting soil and that you can buy organic flowers? "Huh," you might say, or maybe, "Enough already with all this organic stuff." But if you recognize the value of organic food—to your health, to the environment's health, and to the farm workers' health—buying organic potting soil for either your houseplants or perhaps, more importantly, for your vegetable garden, makes a lot of sense. Organic potting soil doesn't contain pesticide and fertilizer residue, ergo better for your houseplants or the vegetables you grow in it. In addition, this soil is much richer in natural nutrients and minerals, as it hasn't been chemically enhanced and "propped up." The vegetables or houseplants you grow in this soil will be more resilient and the former more nutritious to eat.

Now, what about organic flowers? Even more far fetched? The cut flower industry uses huge amounts of fertilizer, fungicides and pesticides, the same way conventional agriculture does for growing produce. Furthermore, when the cut flowers come from outside the U.S.—and most cut flowers in this country are imported from huge Central American cut flower farms—they were likely grown with chemicals that have been banned in this country for their high toxicity. These poisonous chemicals leech into the soil and groundwater, are lethal to bees and other pollinators, and are of course toxic for the farm workers. We are less aware of this problem because it happens so far away, but it's worth a thought.

Why heirlooms?   October 17, 2014

Heirloom fruit and vegetables are older varieties that will reproduce exactly the same kind of plant again from its seeds (hybrids can't). Biodiversity is also a very important reason to choose heirlooms over hybrids (and let me not even mention the "g" word), as we need as many plant varieties around as possible, and especially those that grow well under specific local or strained weather conditions. As a matter of fact, I read somewhere that Peruvians have almost as many potato and corn varieties as growing places, because these plants were all developed for very specific local conditions, and would not perform as well if planted elsewhere. Now that is biodiversity!

In addition, heirlooms are often more disease resistant and have more intense flavors—think deeply flavorful strawberry or tomato instead of the watery, spongy supermarket kinds. There are now even seed libraries to preserve heirloom varieties for future use and generations. Sometimes you can draw from them, but you have to return seeds at the end of the season in exchange for your loan. Lastly, it is infinitely more interesting to taste many different pepper, or tomato, or apple, or carrot kinds (love the purple carrots) than the one or two same old, same old you get at the supermarket.

Hybrids, in comparison, while having some desirable characteristics, can't reproduce from their seeds—think of seedless watermelons or grapes.

And, by the way, heirloom breeds exist among animals as well, and some farmers are now bringing these older breeds back for the same reasons heirloom produce is so desirable.

Yummy soil   November 4, 2014

Big-food (the industrial food producers) attempts to compare the difference between organic and non-organic food by asking the wrong questions (on purpose)—whether organics taste any different than non-organics, and whether there is a difference in the nutritional content. Taste-wise, there may or may not be much of a difference. Regarding the nutritional content, if you simply count the calories and other building blocks, you may not find that much of a difference either. The most important difference between organic, biodynamic (a sort of über-organic), and conventional has to do with soil and micronutrients.

For one, non-organic, conventional produce has pesticide residue on the outside. But perhaps more importantly, conventional produce grows in depleted soil that must be enhanced with chemical fertilizer. And to top if off (pun intended), the topical fungicides, pesticides, and herbicides all seep into the soil. The produce then absorbs this chemical cocktail through the roots, which becomes part and parcel of the produce you eat, an issue the two questions above diplomatically leave aside.

Soil that gets enhanced naturally with manure and compost is inherently much richer in minerals and trace elements, and devoid of chemical toxins. You know if you have such soil in your home garden if it is dark, and crumbly, and full of happy, little creepy crawlies. It should look like Mississippi Mud Pie. Produce that grows in such Mississippi Mud Pie soil is much richer in minerals and trace elements. It is this richness that makes food grown in such soil packed with real nutritional value. Not only is it much more nourishing, we also need to eat less of it (!) to feel satisfied. No empty calories here.

So even though our soil has been depleting steadily with the advent and the spreading of industrial agriculture over the past hundred or so years, it is still better for our health to opt for organically, or better yet biodynamically, grown produce and grains.

What the heck is kernza? November 15, 2014

You might ask what the heck *kernza* is. It's about sustainable agriculture. In short, *sustainable* means *eternally renewable from within*, that is, without bringing outside products in.

We almost take for granted the annual winter seed buying ritual from seed catalogs. And I always thought that buying those decorative annuals for the garden was a bit of a waste, compared to perennials that come up every year again, no worries, no money, no effort. Wouldn't it be nice if our wheat came up every year again? No buying seeds, no sowing, no tilling, less effort, less money. Researchers have been working on exactly that—developing perennial varieties of our staple cereals, and kernza is one of them.

This is thinking more in terms of permaculture, a perennial polyculture, which is what most ecosystems look like, as Mark Bittman explains in a recent article. "In perennial polyculture, the plants may fertilize one another, physically support one another, ward off pests and diseases together, resist drought and flood, and survive even when one member suffers." How does that sound for a wonderfully cooperative plant community? No Darwin here.

Our unsung heroes August 25, 2015

In the end how much does an investment banker's work really contribute to my quality of life? *Nada.* Same goes for a real estate developer's work, a professional athlete's work (some people may disagree, but I believe certain professional athletes are vastly overpaid for what they do), and many other overpaid and overvalued jobs that we have come to admire simply because they earn lots of money.

Instead, I'd like to sing an ode to our unsung heroes, the farmers. They are generally underpaid and overworked for the long hours they work and the incredible risks they have to take year after year. Yet without them we are nothing, not even alive. "No farms, no food," the bumper sticker goes. Weather conditions are a real gamble and constant source of worry for farmers. Wet or dry summers mean less money. And what about several-year droughts? What about the difficult decisions between new technologies and true sustainability? Or the question of whether bigger is better? Farmers simply don't get credited or appreciated for the importance of their work.

Many pioneering young farmers do this job out of conviction and passion for a better world, and unfortunately have to work for a pittance. The government should be giving away farmland to willing and qualified farmers to encourage farming in areas with a sustainable climate (maybe not out West any longer). Why not subsidize small farms, sustainable farms, organic farms, or new farmers? That would acknowledge the value of the farmers' life-sustaining function.

We ought to thank our farmers, we ought to celebrate them, and we need to support them.